Swan Theatre

D1543803

# THE TWO NOBLE KINSMEN
## by William Shakespeare and John Fletcher

A programme/text with commentary by Simon Trussler

Swan Theatre Plays published by Methuen London
by arrangement with the Royal Shakespeare Company

methuen

# RSC
## Swan Theatre

The Swan Theatre is the newest of the Royal Shakespeare Company's five theatres but occupies that part of the original Shakespeare Memorial Theatre which survived the disastrous fire of 1926. The 800-seat Victorian Gothic Stratford Memorial Theatre, opened in 1879, had been built with funds raised in a national campaign led by local brewer Charles Edward Flower, who also generously donated the theatre's famous riverside site. In the years that followed its opening, Stratford-upon-Avon, long celebrated as Shakespeare's birthplace, also became a centre of Shakespearean performance.

Sir Frank Benson, who directed over thirty of the theatre's first fifty seasons, expressed his aims in 1905 in terms which remain relevant to today's Royal Shakespeare Company: 'to train a company, every member of which would be an essential part of a homogenous whole, consecrated to the practice of the dramatic arts and especially to the representation of the plays of Shakespeare'.

When, just a year after the granting, in 1925, of its Royal Charter, the theatre was almost completely destroyed by fire, a worldwide campaign was launched to build a new one. Productions moved to a local cinema until the new theatre, designed by Elisabeth Scott, was opened by the Prince of Wales on 23 April, 1932. Over the next thirty years, under the influence of directors such as Robert Atkins, Bridges-Adams, Iden Payne, Komisarjevsky, Sir Barry Jackson and Anthony Quayle, the Shakespeare Memorial Theatre maintained a worldwide reputation.

In 1960, the newly appointed artistic director, Peter Hall, extended the re-named Royal Shakespeare Company's operations to include a London base at the Aldwych Theatre, and widened the Company's repertoire to include modern as well as classical work. Other innovations of the period which have shaped today's Company were the travelling Theatregoround and experimental work which included the Theatre of Cruelty season.

Under Trevor Nunn, who took over as artistic director in 1968, this experimental work in small performance spaces led, in 1974, to the opening of The Other Place, Stratford-upon-Avon.

This was a rehearsal space converted into a theatre and in 1977 its London counterpart, The Warehouse, opened with a policy of presenting new British plays. In the same year the RSC played its first season in Newcastle upon Tyne – now an annual event.In 1978, the year in which Terry Hands joined Trevor Nunn as artistic director, the RSC also fulfilled an ambition to tour to towns and villages with little or no access to live professional theatre.

In 1982, the RSC moved its London base to the Barbican Centre in the City of London, opening both the Barbican Theatre, specially built for the RSC by the generosity of the Corporation of the City of London, and The Pit, a small theatre converted like The Warehouse and The Other Place, from a rehearsal room.

Throughout its history, the RSC has augmented its central operations with national and international tours, films, television programmes, commercial transfers and fringe activities. Now, in the Swan Theatre, thanks to an extremely generous gift by an anonymous benefactor, the Company is able to explore the vast, popular output of Shakespeare's contemporaries and the period 1570-1750.

Despite box office figures, which, it is thought, have no equal anywhere in the world, the costs of RSC repertoire activities cannot be recouped from ticket sales alone. We rely on assistance from the Arts Council of Great Britain, amounting to about 40 per cent of our costs in any one year, from work in other media and, increasingly, on revenue from commercial sponsorship. To find out more about the RSC's activities and to make sure of priority booking for productions, why not become a member of the Company's Mailing List? For details of how to apply, please contact: Mailing List, Royal Shakespeare Theatre, Stratford-upon-Avon, Warwickshire CV37 6BB. Telephone: (0789) 205301.

**RSC**

**Swan Theatre**

## CAST

for the first public performance of this
RSC production on 26 April 1986.

| | |
|---|---|
| Theseus *Duke of Athens* | **Peter Guinness** |
| Hippolyta *Queen of the Amazons* | **Anna Nygh** |
| Emilia *her sister* | **Amanda Harris** |
| Pirithous *friend of Theseus* | **Robert Morgan** |
| First Queen ⎫ *widows of Kings* | **Rosalind Boxall** |
| Second Queen ⎬ *killed in the* | **Jenni George** |
| Third Queen ⎭ *Siege of Thebes* | **Lucy Hancock** |
| Artesius *an Athenian soldier* | **Philip Sully** |
| Palamon ⎤ *the two* | **Gerard Murphy** |
| Arcite ⎦ *noble kinsmen* | **Hugh Quarshie** |
| Valerius *a Theban* | **John Patrick** |
| The Gaoler *of Theseus' prison* | **Robert Demeger** |
| Gaoler's Daughter | **Imogen Stubbs** |
| The Wooer *of Gaoler's Daughter* | **Donald McBride** |
| First Countryman | **Max Gold** |
| Second Countryman | **John Patrick** |
| Third Countryman | **Philip Sully** |
| Gerrold *a schoolmaster, in charge of the Morris* | **Richard Moore** |
| Countrywomen | **Rosalind Boxall** |
| | **Jenni George** |
| | **Lucy Hancock** |
| A Doctor | **Richard Moore** |
| Brother of Gaoler | **Max Gold** |
| Friends of Gaoler | **John Patrick** |
| | **Philip Sully** |
| Hymen/The Bavian/ The Messenger/The Executioner | **Joseph Mydell** |
| Boys | **James Lowrey** |
| | **Robert Willey** |

Other parts played by members of the company

## MUSICIANS

| | |
|---|---|
| flute/alto flute/piccolo | **Ian Reynolds** |
| bassoon/keyboard | **Roger Hellyer** |
| horn | **Peter Morris** |
| horn | **David Statham** |
| percussion | **Nigel Garvey** |
| harp | **Brynmor Williams/** |
| | **Audrey Douglas** |

| | |
|---|---|
| Directed by | **Barry Kyle** |
| Designed by | **Bob Crowley** |
| Movement by | **Ben Benison** |
| Music by | **Guy Woolfenden** |
| Lighting by | **Wayne Dowdeswell** |
| Company voice work by | **RSC Voice Department** |
| Music Director | **Roger Hellyer** |
| Sound by | **Mo Weinstock** |
| Design Assistant | **Jill Jowett** |
| Stage Manager | **Richard Oriel** |
| Deputy Stage Manager | **Chantal Hauser** |
| Assistant Stage Manager | **Jan Bevis Hughes/** |
| | **Sarah Myatt** |

This performance is approximately 3 hours long
including one interval of 20 minutes.

**Please do not smoke or use cameras or tape recorders
in the auditorium. And please remember that noise
such as whispering, coughing, rustling programmes
and the bleeping of digital watches can be distracting
to performers and also spoils the performance
for other members of the audience.**

Arts Council Funde

**Swan Theatre**

## Royal Shakespeare Company

Incorporated under Royal Charter as the
Royal Shakespeare Theatre
*Patron* Her Majesty The Queen
*President* Lord Wilson
*Deputy President* Sir Kenneth Cork
*Chairman of the Council* Geoffrey A Cass
*Vice Chairman* Dennis L Flower
*Joint Artistic Directors* Terry Hands Trevor Nunn
*Direction* Peggy Ashcroft John Barton Peter Brook
Terry Hands Trevor Nunn
*Consultant Director* Sir Peter Hall

## Swan Theatre

Siobhan Bracke *Casting*
Wayne Dowdeswell *Chief Electrician*
Josie Horton *Deputy Wardrobe Mistress*
Geoff Locker *Production Manager*
Andy Matthews *Deputy Chief Electrician*
Philip Medcraft *Master Carpenter*
Janet Morrow *Publicity*
Nicola Russell *Press (0789) 296655*
Mo Weinstock *Sound*

## Production Credits for The Two Noble Kinsmen

Scenery, painting, properties, costumes and wigs
made in RST Workshops, Stratford-upon-Avon.
Lighting equipment designed and installed by
Leisuretec Engineering, Bracknell. Magic advice
by The Great Kovari. Production photographs by
Stephen Macmillan.

## Facilities

In addition to bar and coffee facilities on the
ground floor, there is wine on sale on the first floor
bridge outside Gallery 1. Toilets, including
facilities for disabled people, are situated on the
ground floor only.

## RSC Collection

Each year the RSC Collection presents a theatre
exhibition associated with the season's plays. This
year's exhibition, to celebrate the opening of the
new Swan, concentrates on the changing styles of
staging from medieval times to the present day.
Come and see our exhibition; browse in the sales
and refreshments area – and book a backstage tour.

## Swan Theatre Repertoire 1986

**The Two Noble Kinsmen**
by William Shakespeare
and John Fletcher

From 15 May
**Every Man In His Humour**
by Ben Jonson

From 3 July
**The Rover**
by Aphra Behn

From September
**The Fair Maid of the West**
by Thomas Heywood

# Commentary

Compiled by Simon Trussler

# Contents

# Director's Note

*The Two Noble Kinsmen* has for a long time been a victim of speculation about its joint-authorship. Published initially in the complete works of Beaumont and Fletcher, the later judgement that Shakespeare had collaborated with Fletcher led to much consigning of the worst passages to Fletcher. A few years ago I directed *The Maid's Tragedy*, a proven work of Beaumont and Fletcher, and could not bring myself to be much interested in the game of who wrote which bit. The job is to try to make the play work as the product of a single dramatic imagination. This may lead to the cutting of stray material by both writers which doesn't contribute to the joint effort.

I initially found this speculation about *The Two Noble Kinsmen* irrelevant, until rehearsing it with the actors when I felt I was more and more hearing the voice of Shakespeare. Certainly the first scene reminded me of a production of *A Midsummer Night's Dream* being hi-jacked by a production of *Macbeth*; certainly the influence of Ophelia on the Gaoler's Daughter was unmistakable; but I more and more felt that this was one of Shakespeare's last plays – even if somebody else had written it with him. I can't prove it of course. But it gave me a goal. I felt that what has appeared to be an unfocused play mixing up tragic conflicts with morris dancing, is organic. It's not a mixture, it's a compound. So I've tried to help by cutting about 350 lines, and striking a new balance. The longer scenes are not always saying more, so I've cut. Act One contains a lot of clotted language – I've tried to make it more speakable by editing. Undramatic repetitions have gone.

Scholars have observed the play seems not to have had a final revision by the authors. I agree with that, and have attempted to tying of some loose ends. Like the gardener, I hope the pruning strengthens the plant.

*Barry Kyle*

## A Plan for the Swan

*It was in the mid-seventies that an ambitious scheme was first put forward to convert the existing burnt-out shell of the old Shakespeare Memorial Theatre into the new Swan Theatre. It was not until the mid-eighties, however, that this dream of the RSC's Artistic Directorate was to become a reality with the inauguration of the Swan in April 1986 and the opening of* The Two Noble Kinsmen. *In an early memorandum outlining a policy for the new theatre Trevor Nunn wrote:*

Since the idea of the Swan was first conceived, it was accompanied by the twin notion of what should be its repertoire. John Napier was first commissioned in 1978 to design an auditorium inside the shell of the Conference Hall: the architectural nature of the new theatre and the parameters of its repertoire were to be indivisible. Michael Reardon, the architect, is now in the process of fulfilling this original brief, and a custom-built theatre, in the most precise sense of the term, is nearing completion – a theatre for the performance of sixteenth, seventeenth and eighteenth-century plays which can be seen as broadly contextual to our house dramatist, William Shakespeare.

Since 1964 we had agreed that in an ideal world we should be doing one play a year by Shakespeare's contemporaries, and we did indeed produce in the main house *The Duchess of Malfi, Women Beware Women, The Jew of Malta, The Revenger's Tragedy* and *Dr Faustus*. However, the worsening overall financial position of the Company decreed that we could no longer afford the comparatively lower box-office response for the annual non-Shakespeare.

Naturally the inauguration of The Other Place provided us with a space for alternatives to Shakespeare, as much as for alternatives to the methods and values of the international cultural centre which the

Royal Shakespeare Company had become. So, as a Company, we have almost continuously responded to the imperative of presenting examples of the plays which might have influenced Shakespeare, or the plays which he might have influenced, or the plays which give us, both practitioners and audiences, greater insight into sixteenth and seventeenth-century England.

In the process, we have revealed the existence of several minor masterpieces, we have discovered several exceptions to the 'genres' that scholars might have led us to expect, we have proved that 'neglected' works can still provide tremendous entertainment and theatrical excitement, and we have proved that Shakespeare was surrounded by approaches to dramaturgy which were almost certainly experimental and which can lay claim to being considered more modern and comprehensible to us than his own. And we have only scratched the surface.

There remain countless plays that have continued dormant and which deserve our attention. We have only touched the obvious Marlowe plays, we have never explored the Shakespeare apocrypha, and (bordering on disgrace) we have only ever attempted three plays by Ben Jonson, who in any other language would be the national playwright and have a theatre devoted to him. We have scarcely visited the sixteenth century before Shakespeare, we have never done a masque, and it is high time we tested received ideas about the Restoration, since there would seem to be at least as many exceptions as there are rules.

Of necessity, the key to the whole operation is that the interior design of the theatre amounts to a permanent staging. There is a promontory stage, and back wall that continues the galleried features of the auditorium to provide a sense of upper and inner stage, without amounting to an attempt to 'recreate' the Globe or even the original Swan. It is the simplest possible structure on which we can present the pre-proscenium plays of our dramatic tradition. It is a theatre for texts and actors, for the work of analysis, structure, insight and performance. Clearly, design will have a vital significance in what we do there, but it cannot be design involving changing the configuration of the stage, or even of 'set building' in the sense that we currently understand it.

The task is to prove that these plays live, not that they can be preserved in aspic. And in terms of the first few years at the Swan the task is to communicate and insist on the special identity of the theatre and its policy. So the very first year must not only observe the policy but expound and extol it.

I propose that we should do four plays. One from the Shakespeare apocrypha to establish the link with the main house and the contextual bearing; one early Elizabethan or pre-Shakespearean play to establish the breadth of the territory we are to investigate; one neglected classic from Shakespeare's Elizabethan or Jacobean contemporaries; and one play from the late-seventeenth or early-eighteenth century, to define the opposite bank.

## Sources and Stage History

The main plot of *The Two Noble Kinsmen*, which had already been utilized in two lost Elizabethan plays, is borrowed from the first of Chaucer's *Canterbury Tales*, 'The Knight's Tale', which was in turn quite closely derived from the *Teseida* of Boccaccio. Unusually, the debt to Chaucer is acknowledged in the play's prologue. The first act, supposedly by Shakespeare, adheres much less strictly to its original than the Fletcherian middle acts, but the story is rendered with greater fidelity than Shakespeare paid to most of his sources. Chaucer's expansive time-span is, however, more tightly managed here, and the thematic emphasis shifts from suffering patiently endured to the workings of chance and fortune.

The morris dance in Act III, Scene v, was borrowed from *The Masque of the Inner Temple and Gray's Inn* by Fletcher's erstwhile collaborator, Francis Beaumont. As this had been presented before James I on 20 February 1613, its use gives us the probable earliest date for the play, and if the 'losses' which are said to 'fall so thick' for the company in the prologue include, as seems likely, the burning-down of the Globe on 29 June, a first performance at the Blackfriars early in the winter season on 1613-14 is indicated. The play was not printed until the quarto of 1634, after the deaths of both Fletcher and Shakespeare, who were jointly credited with the authorship on its title page. However, after 1679 it was included in collected editions of the plays of Beaumont and Fletcher.

Allusions to the play in Ben Jonson's *Bartholomew Fair*, first performed on 31 October 1614, suggest that it was by then well-known to audiences; and Revels Office records, together with the use of minor actors' names in the quarto text, suggest revivals around 1620 and 1625. After the Restoration the play reached the stage only in the adaptation made by Sir William Davenant as *The Rivals*, performed at Drury Lane in 1664, with Betterton as the Palamon-figure Philander, who in this version ends up marrying the daughter of the jailer, himself promoted to provost. There are no records of subsequent productions until the present century, when Andrew Leigh directed the play for the Old Vic Company on 12 March 1928, with Eric Portman as Arcite and Ernest Milton as Palamon. There were later revivals during the Shakespeare Quatercentenary Festival at the Bristol Old Vic in 1964; at the Theatre Royal, York, in 1973; and – the single post-war professional production in London – at the Open Air Theatre in Regents Park on 31 July 1974, directed by Mervyn Willis. The play has never before been produced by the Royal Shakespeare Company.

## Synopsis

On the day planned for his wedding to Hippolyta, Duke Theseus of Athens is petitioned by three queens to go to war against King Creon of Thebes, who has deprived their dead husbands of proper burial rites. In Thebes, the 'two noble kinsmen', Palamon and Arcite, realize that their own hatred for Creon's tyranny must be put aside while their native city is in danger, but in spite of their valour in battle, it is Theseus who is victorious. Imprisoned in Athens, the cousins catch sight of Hippolyta's sister Emilia, and both fall instantly in love with her. Arcite is set free, but disguises himself rather than return to Thebes, while Palamon escapes with the help of the Gaoler's Daughter, who loves him. Encountering each other, the kinsmen agree that mortal combat between them must decide the issue; but they are discovered by Theseus, who is persuaded to revoke his sentence of death, and instead decrees that a tournament shall decide which of the cousins is to be married to the indecisive Emilia, which to lose his head. The Gaoler's Daughter has meanwhile been driven mad by her unrequited love, but she accepts her former suitor when he pretends to be Palamon, and seems sure of recovery. Before the tournament, Arcite makes a lengthy invocation to Mars, while Palamon prays to Venus, and Emilia to Diana – for victory to go to the one who loves her best. Although Arcite triumphs, he is thrown from his horse before the death sentence on Palamon can be carried out, and with his last breath bequeathes Emilia to his friend.

## Aspects of Collaborative Authorship

Collaborative authorship was by no means unusual in the theatre of Shakespeare's day. Even before the opening of the permanent play-houses, the play often described as the first English tragedy, *Gorboduc* (1565), was a joint work by Thomas Norton and Thomas Sackville, while no fewer than eight writers were credited with a share in another early tragedy, *The Misfortunes of Arthur* (1588). A great many of the plays written before 1590 appeared anonymously – just as the authorship of much medieval literature remains unknown – and may have been in part the product of 'collective creation' and of oral accretion.

With the rise of the professional theatre, most dramatists wrote with the needs of particular companies and the skills of specific actors in mind; to share the writing was not necessarily a matter of pressing deadlines or economic necessity, but simply an aspect of what has always been the collaborative process of play production. Gerald Eades Bentley has calculated that of the fifteen hundred or so plays which we know at least by name between 1590 and 1642, three hundred and seventy were of unknown authorship, while some twenty per cent of the remainder included a contribution from more than one dramatist. The actual proportion was probably higher, for the more detailed information available from the records of the manager Philip Henslowe suggests that only one-third of the plays presented by the Admiral's and Worcester's Men were the work of a single playwright. Payments are recorded by Henslowe to up to five writers for a single play.

Only occasionally (and then accidentally) are the precise shares of such work directly attributable, other than on stylistic or linguistic evidence. We happen to know that Ben Jonson was not personally responsible for the offensive jokes against King James's fellow-Scotsmen that landed his two collaborators on *Eastward Ho!* in prison, because he showed the solidarity of joining them there voluntarily. Jonson was unique among his fellows in the scrupulous care he took over the printing of his plays: he was careful to record that *Volpone* had been written 'without a co-adjutor', and that although 'a second pen had good share' in *Sejanus*, Jonson had substituted new lines of his own for the published version.

John Fletcher's collaboration with Francis Beaumont began around 1608, and lasted until the latter's marriage to an heiress in 1613 – around the time of Fletcher's supposed association with Shakespeare. The names of Beaumont and Fletcher became so inseparably linked that the collected *Comedies and Tragedies* published in 1647 retained the joint attribution, although at least 30 of the 52 plays included were written after Beaumont's death. Massinger has most frequently been nominated as Fletcher's alternative co-author, but the hands of Rowley, Field, and Shirley have also been discerned by literary detectives. Rowley, like John Ford, wrote mostly in collaboration, and this pair joined with

Thomas Dekker in 1621 to produce *The Witch of Edmonton*, revived by the RSC in 1981. As in this case, a number of collaborations were seemingly dictated by the need to get a play staged before its topical appeal declined: but the main impulse for collaboration was surely an unconscious recognition that the playwright had the very spelling of his occupation in common with other *makers of goods*: he was concerned with a shared theatrical craft, not an exclusive literary art, and saw no reason to be ashamed of that.

---

'We are given clearly enough, a life in two stages: youth, in which the passion of spontaneous friendship is dominant, and the riper age in which there is a dominant sexual passion, leading to marriage where it can. The movement from one stage to the next, the unavoidable process of growth, is a movement away from innocence, away from joy.'

*Philip Edwards (1964)*

'In Shakespeare's choice of *The Knight's Tale* as a subject for a play, we can see that same return to earlier subjects which is apparent in the choice of stories for *Pericles, Cymbeline,* and *The Winter's Tale*. The use of Chaucer parallels that of Gower in *Pericles*, of the old romantic play, *The Rare Triumphs of Love and Fortune,* in *Cymbeline*, and of Greene's *Pandosto* in *The Winter's Tale*. The sense of return to earlier interests is reinforced by the connection of Theseus and his wedding with *A Midsummer Night's Dream,* and the resemblance between Emilia's description of her friendship with Flavina and the friendship of Helena and Hermia as Helena describes it. The story of Palamon and Arcite requires dramatic handling of the theme of love and friendship, which Shakespeare had not made central to any play since *The Two Gentlemen of Verona* . . .'

*Richard Proudfoot (1966)*

'In Chaucer's *Knight's Tale* the outcome of a combat for a lady depends on enlisting the right gods as backer; Palamon prefers Venus to Mars and is rewarded with eventual victory. Yet this apparently meaningless denouement is taken by Shakespeare for a major part of his contribution, and the themes he announces in his first act suggest the significance he saw in an ancient story. Theseus on his wedding-day is begged by three queens to redeem their husbands' corpses from tyrannous Creon; the spheres of Mars and Venus, as they will be defined by the knights' invocations before battle, are in immediate opposition. . . . The battle stands for a larger conflict. Neither the values of Mars nor those of Diana are rejected, yet both are seen to be at the mercy of Venus . . .'

*David L. Frost (1968)*

# 'The Kinsmen' and the King's Men

Paul Bertram suggests that *The Two Noble Kinsmen* was written in some haste after the fire which destroyed the first Globe Theatre on 29 June 1613, during a performance of Shakespeare and Fletcher's *Henry VIII*. Probably it was first performed during the King's Men's winter season at the Blackfriars, during which the Globe was rebuilt – 'in far fairer manner than before' – in time for reopening by June 1614.

Since 1610 – after two years in which the plague had prevented playing during the summer months – the company had been regularly dividing its year between two theatres, which attracted rather different kinds of audience. The Globe was situated in the traditional entertainment district on the Bankside, in close proximity to brothels and bear-baiting as well as to other open-air or 'public' playhouses such as the Rose, the original Swan, and later the Hope. Now, it was playing only in the summer, when the aristocracy was out-of-town and the Inns of Court were on vacation. Here the 'groundlings' could be crowded into the pit-area or yard around the projecting apron stage, without seats or protection from the weather, and although the encircling tiered galleries provided better accommodation at a higher price (it was apparently their thatched covering which allowed the fire of 1613 to take hold) more affluent citizens increasingly preferred the indoor or 'private' theatres.

The Blackfriars, converted into an indoor playhouse from parts of the old Dominican Priory between Ludgate Hill and the Thames, was the first of these so-called 'private' theatres to be used by adult rather than boy players. Prices were higher in this smaller, more comfortable house, which accordingly became the preserve of more select audiences. Here, a seat on the pit-benches was actually more expensive than a place in the galleries, from which the 'end-on' staging made for a more restricted view.

*The Two Noble Kinsmen* is one of only two extant plays known to have been written for performance at the Blackfriars during the tenure of the King's Men – the other being one of the collaborations between Beaumont and Fletcher, *The Maid's Tragedy*. Despite the more demanding technical effects which such 'indoor' plays often seem to demand, the repertoires of the company's two theatres were in practice interchangeable, and whatever social distinctions separated their audiences, tastes in plays do not seem to have divided along lines of class. The social composition of Shakespeare's audiences has, admittedly, been the subject of much recent scholarly debate: what is indisputable is the overwhelming importance of the works of the two collaborators on *The Two Noble Kinsmen* in the repertoire of the King's Men around this time.

Thus, Richard Proudfoot has calculated that between 1606 and 1613 there is evidence that the company presented some forty plays, of which five are now lost (one of these a collaboration between Shakespeare and Fletcher, *Cardenio*, also performed in 1613). No less than twelve of the extant remainder were written by Shakespeare alone (including revivals of earlier works), and he had at least a collaborative share in a further three – with Fletcher on *Henry VIII* and *The Two Noble Kinsmen*, and in *Pericles*. John Fletcher worked in his better-known (though much exaggerated) collaboration with Francis Beaumont on *Philaster*, *The Maid's Tragedy*, *A King and No King*, and *The Captain*, and contributed two plays entirely from his own hand, *Bonduca* and *Valentinian* – an active start indeed to the role of the company's chief dramatist which he assumed on Shakespeare's retirement.

---

'There is a series of mad scenes in the subplot . . . which descend from Ophelia's, but have Fletcher's peculiar nastiness. In another disastrous passage the noble youths Palamon and Arcite break off urgent business to discuss old conquests with the vain salacity of saloon-bar amorists. This sorts ill with certain protestations Palamon later makes to Venus. *Two Noble Kinsmen*, with its flippant Prologue and Epilogue, belongs in some ways to a later age than Shakespeare's. The first scene is always attributed to Shakespeare, but it is difficult to believe that he *planned* it, with its slow, falsely posed, ceremonial appeal by the three young queens; indeed, the *ordonnance* of the whole work suggests the peculiar talents of Fletcher.'

*Frank Kermode (1963)*

'The gods of the play are powerful and not clearly benevolent, although just, and temperance and chastity – the key virtues of Shakespeare's scenes in *The Two Noble Kinsmen* as they are of *The Tempest* and its immediate predecessors – are man's best protection in dealing with them. But *The Two Noble Kinsmen* is unlike those plays in that the winning of love and the death of Arcite are juxtaposed at the end so that the overwhelming impression is not so much of the value of love as of its appalling cost.'

*Richard Proudfoot (1966)*

'The Shakespearian scenes of Act V are crowded with allusions to the gods, but the supernatural does not take the form of a kindly providence that reunites the lost and separated. The gods are constantly present but never reveal themselves . . . and the tokens they give to their worshippers are inexplicit and could even be regarded as ironically misleading. . . .'

*N.W.Bawcutt (1977)*

## Chronology: Two Playwrights and their Company

| Shakespeare | The King's Men | Fletcher (to 1616) |
|---|---|---|
| 1564  Born in Stratford-upon-Avon | | |
| | 1574  Act authorizing Master of the Revels to license acting companies | |
| | 1576  The Theatre built, Shoreditch | |
| | | 1579  Born in Rye, Sussex, son of a clergyman who became Bishop of London |
| 1582  Married Anne Hathaway. Their daughter Susanna born | | |
| 1585  Twins Hamnet and Judith born. No further record of his life until 1592 | | |
| | 1586  First recorded performance by Lord Chamberlain's Men | |
| | | 1591  ?Pensioner of Corpus Christi College, Cambridge |
| 1592  *Henry VI, Parts 1-3* and *Richard III* | | |
| 1594  Record of his being paid as leading sharer with Chamberlain's. *The Comedy of Errors, The Taming of the Shrew, Titus Andronicus.* | 1594  Chamberlain's newly formed from members of Strange's-Derby's, playing mainly at The Theatre | 1594  ?Awarded his BA Degree from Cambridge |
| 1595-96  *Two Gentlemen of Verona, Love's Labour's Lost, King John, Richard II, Romeo and Juliet* | | 1596  Death of his father, heavily in debt, leaving 8 children. No more known of Fletcher's life until 1605 |

596-97 Coat of arms granted to Shakespeare's father. *Midsummer Night's Dream, The Merchant of Venice, The Merry Wives of Windsor, Henry IV, Part 1*. Buys New Place in Stratford

1597 Playing at the Curtain, in Bishopsgate

597-98 *Henry IV, Part 2, Much Ado About Nothing*

1598 Jonson's *Every Man in His Humour*

599 *Henry V, As You Like It, Julius Caesar*

1599 Opening of the first Globe Theatre on Bankside. Jonson's *Every Man out of His Humour*

600-01 *Hamlet, Twelfth Night*. Death of his father

1601 Dekker's *Satiromastix*

602 *Troilus and Cressida*

1602 *The Merry Devil of Edmonton*

603 *All's Well that Ends Well*

1603 Death of Elizabeth. Company becomes King's Men under patronage of James I. Jonson's *Sejanus*

604 *Measure for Measure, Othello*

605 *King Lear*

1605 Jonson's *Volpone*

1605 *The Woman's Prize*

606 *Macbeth*

1606 *A Yorkshire Tragedy*, Tourneur's *The Revenger's Tragedy*

607 *Antony and Cleopatra*

608 *Coriolanus, Timon of Athens, Pericles* (possibly in collaboration). Death of his mother

1608 *The Faithful Shepherdess* (for Queen's Revels Children)

609 *Cymbeline*

1609 Blackfriars Theatre becomes winter home of the King's Men. Tourneur's *The Atheist's Tragedy*

1609 Collaboration with Beaumont begins: *Philaster* and *The Coxcomb*

610 Returns to settle in Stratford. *The Winter's Tale*

1610 Jonson's *The Alchemist*

1610 *The Captain* and *The Maid's Tragedy*, both with Beaumont

611 *The Tempest*

1611 Jonson's *Catiline*

1611 *A King and No King* with Beaumont

1612 Twenty plays at Court during celebrations of marriage of James's daughter to Elector Palatine

1612 Marries Joan Herring. Begins the collaboration with Shakespeare?

613 *Henry VIII, The Two Noble Kinsmen*, and the lost *Cardenio* all written with Fletcher?

1613 Globe burned down. First performance of *The Two Noble Kinsmen* at Blackfriars?

1613-15 *The Scornful Lady* with Beaumont, *The Honest Man's Fortune* with Field and Massinger, and *Wit without Money, Monsieur Thomas, Valentinian*, on his own

1614 Second Globe opened. Webster's *The Duchess of Malfi*

616 Death of Shakespeare

1616 Jonson's *The Devil Is an Ass*

1616 *The Mad Lover*

## The Shakespeare Apocrypha

Among the scanty and scattered information we have about Shakespeare's life and opinions is Thomas Heywood's belief, recorded in his *Apology for Actors* (1612), that Shakespeare was 'much offended' with William Jaggard, the publisher who had 'presumed to make so bold with his name' by ascribing the whole edition of the poetic miscellany *The Passionate Pilgrim* to his authorship – although only five of the items included were his work, and those, of course, were pirated. Shakespeare must have been no less annoyed to have his reputation exploited by other unscrupulous publishers, who variously credited him with *The London Prodigal* (1605), *A Yorkshire Tragedy* (1608), and the second edition of *The Troublesome Reign of King John* (1611).

Of the seven plays added to the second impression of the collected folio edition of 1663, only *Pericles* is now generally accepted as Shakespeare's – the others, besides *The London Prodigal* and *A Yorkshire Tragedy*, being *The History of Thomas Lord Cromwell*, *Sir John Oldcastle: Lord Cobham*, *The Puritan*, and *The Lamentable Tragedy of Locrine*. Misattribution was widespread at the time, and three plays bound together in the library of Charles II – *The Merry Devil of Edmonton*, *Mucedorus*, and *Fair Em the Miller's Daughter of Edmonton* – were firmly labelled *Shakespeare Vol. I. Arden of Faversham* and *The Birth of Merlin* were among other spurious ascriptions.

Modern scholars have, however, detected Shakespearian passages in *Edward III* (1596), while three pages of the manuscript of *Sir Thomas More* (unprinted until 1844) have been claimed to be in Shakespeare's own handwriting – stylistic evidence also supporting his probable authorship. For his *The Shakespeare Apocrypha* (1908), C.F.Tucker Brooke excluded *Pericles* (by then beginning to be accepted as part of the undisputed canon), and also *Lord Cobham*, but otherwise assembled all thirteen of the plays previously mentioned – adding to them *The Two Noble Kinsmen*, about which he was, however, extremely sceptical. This collection, alas out of print, but G. R. Proudfoot is presently preparing a critical, old-spelling edition of the apocryphal plays for Oxford University Press.

## Shakespeare, Fletcher, and the Evidences of Authorship

Of the three plays considered by many scholars to be a product of collaboration between Shakespeare and Fletcher, one – *Cardenio*, first performed at the Court of King James during the Christmas celebrations of 1612-13 – exists only in the form of an eighteenth-century version by Lewis Theobald called *Double Falsehood*, acted in 1727 and of unknown provenance. *Henry VIII*, staged at the Globe in the summer season of 1613 – and in performance on 29 June, when over-enthusiastic use of explosives for cannon-fire was the cause of the theatre's burning down – is regarded by some authorities as exclusively Shakespeare's; and certainly any collaboration left fewer signs of ill-butted joints than are to be found in *The Two Noble Kinsmen*. But most critics now agree that this last play is indeed the joint work of the two writers, *one* of whom was surely Fletcher. The identity of the second writer has provided scope for long and ultimately inconclusive debate – of which some contradictory examples appear alongside.

Against the exclusion of *The Two Noble Kinsmen* from the First Folio of Shakespeare's work – printed in 1623 with the authority of the usually dependable Hemming and Condell, Shakespeare's long-time fellow-actors – must be set the unequivocal title-page attribution in the first and only quarto edition of 1634. This, the only external evidence for partial Shakespearian authorship, is, however, supported by an analysis of textual characteristics. The play's earliest editors suggested the division of labours which has generally been accepted, on the basis of such clues as Fletcher's relatively frequent use of 'feminine' (or extra-syllabic) line-endings as compared with the typically 'late-Shakespearian' percentage found in non-Fletcherian scenes. E.K.Chambers also compared the percentage of 'light' and 'weak' endings in Shakespeare's undisputed last plays – *Cymbeline*, *The Winter's Tale*, and *The Tempest* – and found them remarkably close to those of the non-Fletcherian scenes of *The Two Noble Kinsmen*, while an examination of their relative frequency in Shakespeare's other surviving collaboration with Fletcher, *Henry VIII*, showed a strikingly similar pattern. Later tests dealing with matters of vocabulary and word-coinage largely seemed to support the proposed division – that Shakespeare was responsible for Act I, Act V (excluding Scene ii), and for the meeting between the escaped Palamon and Arcite in Act III, Scene i; and Fletcher for the remainder.

But while Marco Mincoff could sum up the evidence in 1952 as beyond reasonable doubt, Una Ellis-Fermor still pronounced persuasively, if largely from gut-instinct, against a Shakespearian share. Richard Proudfoot even suggests the participation of a third author, responsible for the sub-plot of the gaoler's daughter, which, as he points out, is kept completely separate from the main plot, apart from twenty lines in the last act which could well have been interpolated to forge a link elsewhere conspicuously absent. This hypothetical third collaborator is likely to have worked in a similar way to Shakespeare and Fletcher – suggesting an agreed division of labours separately carried out, with only a perfunctory attempt at interlocking when the pieces were put together, in contrast to the closer, more 'organic' collaboration usual when Fletcher was working with Beaumont, and arguably in evidence between Fletcher and Shakespeare in *Henry VIII*.

## Some Contributions to the Authorship Debate

'That Fletcher should have copied Shakespeare's manner through so many entire scenes . . . is not very probable, that he could have done it with such facility is to me not certain. His ideas moved slow; his versification, though sweet, is tedious, it stops every moment; he lays line upon line, making up one after the other, adding image to image so deliberately that we see where they join; Shakespeare mingles every thing, he runs line into line, embarrasses sentences and metaphors; before one idea has burst its shell, another has hatched and is clamorous for disclosure. If Fletcher wrote some scenes in imitation, why did he stop? or shall we say that Shakespeare wrote the other scenes in imitation of Fletcher? that he gave Shakespeare a curb and a bridle, and that Shakespeare gave him a pair of spurs . . .'

*Charles Lamb (1808)*

'No author has been or can be suggested whose style approaches that of the doubtful parts of *The Two Noble Kinsmen* even approximately as closely as Shakespeare's does. On the internal evidence alone Shakespeare remains the only possible candidate. The idea of an epigone, unschooled in philological analysis, imitating the minutiae of Shakespeare's style at a definite period down to the very metrical percentages, capable too of such splendid poetry, yet never apparently repeating the attempt, is too fanciful to need refutation.'

*Marco Mincoff (1952)*

'The persistent shallowness of characterization in Emilia, the superficial novelty in Hippolyta, which never fulfils its promise, the false motivation, the evoking of emotion by undramatic methods – all these cut deeper into the art of the play and reveal habits of thought and technique so unlike Shakespeare's that they have shaken the confidence of many critics who have been convinced or half-convinced by the style. In the same way, the conduct of the plot is unlike that of an artist whose known processes have the economy of great architecture . . .'

*Una Ellis-Fermor (1961)*

'When I went over the play again recently I found myself for a brief period holding four mutually incompatible convictions: first that the play could not possibly be Shakespeare's, second that it was too much like his work to be anyone else's, third that it was the product of an unholy alliance between Chapman and Beaumont, both temporarily intoxicated by Shakespeare's later tragic style, and fourth that it was the only surviving play of an unknown genius who had read nothing for some six weeks but Shakespeare's mature tragedies. Setting aside the more frivolous of these suggestions, I find myself back at the first position, that it cannot possibly be Shakespeare's work.'

*Una Ellis-Fermor (1961)*

'I find it impossible to believe in an unknown poet who wrote great poetry, only distinguishable from Shakespeare's by its excess and continuity of brilliance. . . . Let us assume, however, that this anonymous imitator of Shakespeare did exist. He was (let us say) a young poet of the name of Henry Tomkins who came up to London to study at one of the Inns of Court, and spent all his time in the playhouse, watching Shakespeare's plays. He bribed the prompter to lend him copies of *The Tempest* and *The Winter's Tale*, and began to write *The Two Noble Kinsmen*. He took a few scenes to Burbage, who thought they were promising enough to get Fletcher to collaborate. When Burbage, noticing the Shakespearian flavour of Tomkins's style, asked him how he managed it, the young man explained modestly his methods of composition. He had always admired Shakespeare's work and he had tried to imitate it as closely as possible. He had counted up the percentage of weak-endings and light-endings in his last few plays and had kept to this percentage in his own verse – or rather he had increased the percentage to tally with what Shakespeare might have written in 1613. He had noticed that Shakespeare introduced a word he had not used before every twelve lines and a new coinage every twenty lines; but he decided to coin a new word rather more frequently, since the percentage tended to increase. He had been careful, of course, to draw his images from the same fields as Shakespeare, and in roughly the same proportion. The reason why we hear nothing of Tomkins is that he died of the plague a few months later. I find it very hard to believe in Tomkins.'

*Kenneth Muir (1960)*

## Two Complex Kinsmen

It is unfortunate that literary criticism of *The Two Noble Kinsmen* (there is little enough of it, and for *theatre* criticism there has been almost no opportunity at all) should have been so completely dominated by the debate over authorship. One is tempted to ask the old question: apart from that, Mrs Lincoln, what did you think of the *play*?

Consider: it is proposed that the contrast between the nobility of the kinsmen in Shakespeare's opening act, or of the dedicated pair invoking the deities before the tournament, and what Frank Kermode calls the 'vain salacity of saloon-bar amorists' displayed in Fletcher's share of the action, shows the strain of collective authorship resulting in inconsistent characterization. Yet if we forget all about the collaboration issue, and remember instead Shakespeare's awareness of the gulf between platonic intentions and the temptations of 'available' reality in *Love's Labour's Lost* or *Measure for Measure*; his blunt confrontation with the nastiness beneath the surface of courtly-love assumptions in *The Two Gentlemen of Verona*; Desdemona revealing the pert Cressida beneath the skin on the quayside in *Othello*; or, nearest in time to the present play, Prospero's grim harping in *The Tempest* on how easily young love can sow 'weeds so loathly': then we may suspect that this 'inconsistency' shows a similar precise knowledge of how the male human being adapts his sexual persona to circumstances and pressures.

Thus, the high-flown condemnation by Palamon and Arcite of 'the common stream' of Creon's Thebes fits well enough with their need to rationalize an intended flight. If their subsequent protestations that prison will preserve friendship from the temptations of wives and business ring with an acknowledged irony just before the not-quite-mutual glimpse they catch of Emilia, then why cannot the childish 'I saw her first' be accepted as a flaw of character, not an absurdity of characterization? And no less ironical, surely, is that sudden, much criticized flow of sexual banter, inflamed by wine, meat, and the taste of freedom. Indeed, Palamon's invocation before the altar of Venus, with its elaborate disclaimers of unsavoury sexual meddlings, has a curious ring if it is *not* intended to suggest that this young man protests too much. Well, he would, wouldn't he?

Again: critics seize on the indecisiveness of Emilia as a symptom of one-dimensionality, or the reduction of a character to a function, and claim that the sub-plot of the Gaoler's Daughter lacks any connection with the main theme. Yet wanton wenches from the lower orders who give rein to their sexual inclinations are familiar enough in Shakespeare's plays – and familiarly enough contrasted with high-born ladies who put a proper price on their own virginity. The Gaoler's Daughter is less a mad sister to Ophelia than a tragicomic version of the all-too-available Jaquenetta in *Love's Labour's Lost* – or perhaps a sort of siamese twin from *As You Like It*, combining the honest earthiness of Audrey with the pretensions of poor Phebe, likewise fobbed-off with an inferior substitute for daring to fall in love beyond her social station. Shakespeare's sense of class-consciousness in matters of sexuality and marriage may not today seem particularly admirable, but it is at least consistent.

Of course, this is not to suggest that all the problems raised by collaborative authorship can be so satisfactorily resolved. But we need no more expect that the Shakespeare who probably took a hand in *The Two Noble Kinsmen* should still be at the height of his powers than we need share the conventional modern (but not Jacobean) sense of Fletcher's lowly place among Shakespeare's contemporaries. As N.W.Bawcutt has pointed out, at this stage of his career Shakespeare would, indeed, have been far likelier to prove a sympathetic collaborator with Fletcher than with Webster or Middleton, whose plays better suit our own sensibilities. We understand the jaded world of *The White Devil* better than the comical-tragical-pastoral possibilities of *The Winter's Tale*, dressed up in better poetry though it is. We can enter into the claustrophobic, Kafkaesque castle of *The Revenger's Tragedy* more readily than we can join that reconciliatory voyage on which the characters of *The Tempest* are about to embark. But Shakespeare, being Shakespeare, knew that whatever the expectations of the romantic taste for which he learned to cater, Caliban lived, and Ferdinand probably lusted despite his best intentions. Whether or not the sudden hatred and the unexpected sensuality of Palamon and Arcite reveal the hand of Fletcher scarcely matters, so long as they render a sense of that cussedness and complexity which, despite decorum, Shakespeare knew to be inseparable from the human condition under stress.

'Such thought as the play has, which is far less than it appears to have, lacks altogether that depth, that simultaneous hold upon intellect and imagination, which we recognize in any work of Shakespeare's designing. There is at once more explicit statement alike of sentiment and of reflection and less implication of coherent reading of life than we find in the total impression of *Pericles* or even *Timon*. Fake values at work in the underlying thought emerge in the characters as false motivation, to reinforce the theatrical tone of the situations and the episodic nature of the structure. And all these weaknesses are screened by a bewildering brilliance of style and a facile and dexterous release of the shallower emotions. It is hardly worth while to search behind this screen for a theme, and still less for a valid relation between theme and subject – that ultimate test of dramatic virility.'

*Una Ellis-Fermor (1961)*

## 'Tragi-Comedy' and its Conventions

Although we may be tempted to group *The Two Noble Kinsmen* with Shakespeare's other last plays as 'romances', this was not a term much used by his contemporaries in relation to the theatre. And Polonius's famous catalogue of dramatic permutations in *Hamlet* (*c*.1600) does not even include tragi-comedy as such. Indeed, it was only after 1609 that the form really came into fashion, when the emergent partnership of Beaumont and Fletcher coincided with the opening of the Blackfriars as winter quarters for the King's Men, and the consequent need for plays to attract its more courtly-minded audiences. The fact that plays with widely differing origins came to be collected into the Beaumont and Fletcher 'canon' suggests how closely the partnership was identified with this particular kind of playwriting: and the popularity of tragi-comedy increased rather than diminished after Beaumont's death, for in the years between 1616 and the closing of the theatres by the puritans in 1642, no less than 47 of the plays from this 'canon' featured in the repertoire of the King's Men, compared with a mere sixteen of Shakespeare's and nine of Ben Jonson's out of a repertoire of around 170. Significantly, the proportion of tragi-comedies in performances at court was even higher.

L.G. Salingar succinctly summed up the characteristic movement of plays like *Philaster* and *A King and No King* (both *c*.1610), which 'commonly pass from a mysterious quarrel or disappearance, through episodes of concealed identity and mistaken purpose, to the moment of discovery that brings about the triumphant denouement.' Leaving aside the moral judgements critics often proceed to pass on such plays, which they view as symptomatic of the decadence of later Jacobean and Caroline drama, it's certainly true that this describes the drift of *Cymbeline* or *The Winter's Tale* as much as of *The Two Noble Kinsmen*. But it's no less reminiscent of one of Shakespeare's very earliest comedies – possibly his first, written in the early 1590s, long before the vogue for tragi-comedy set in: and even the title of *The Two Gentlemen of Verona* is reminiscent of our play. Here again are two close male friends who believe that their friendship surpasses that of man for woman, and who, sure enough, eventually fall out after falling in love with the same woman – but are reconciled when one of them offers the other the woman he loves, without even the excuse that he's dying at the time. This theme of the friendship of Palamon and Arcite is given greater prominence in *The Two Noble Kinsmen* by the parallel stress on the love of Theseus and Pirithous, which it is Hippolyta's superior skill to have 'parted' without creating jealousy.

It was not, of course, upsetting to the decorum of Jacobean drama that characters should fall in love after the briefest distant glimpse, and without a second thought (except perhaps to assure themselves of the chosen lady's financial status). And the means by which the suitor to the jailer's daughter here consummates his desires is no less conventional – just another variation, indeed, on the 'bed trick' of the substituted lover, already used by Shakespeare to couple characters of superior birth in *Measure for Measure* and *All's Well That Ends Well*. Far from imagining that Shakespeare's last plays are some sort of dramatic equivalent to the late quartets of Beethoven, then, they may simply be the work of a pragmatic dramatist well in tune with his audience's developing tastes. The truth, of course, probably lies somewhere in between – just as the product of his collaboration with Fletcher here effects neither a complete failure nor a complete success but, at the very least, creates some intriguing dramatic tensions, in which well-used Shakespearian conventions are caught up in a newly-popular form.

## For Further Reading

The text of the play was first edited by Harold Littledale in three parts for the New Shakspere Society (London, 1876 and 1885). It is by no means invariably included in modern critical editions of Shakespeare's works, but good scholarly texts have been edited by Clifford Leech for the Signet Shakespeare (New York, 1966); by G.R. Proudfoot for the Regents Renaissance Drama Series (Lincoln, Nebraska, and London, 1970), and by N.W. Bawcutt for the New Penguin Shakespeare (Harmondsworth, 1977). Kenneth Muir surveys the various earlier opinions on the play's authorship in his *Shakespeare as Collaborator* (London: Methuen, 1960); while a later work, Paul Bertram's *Shakespeare and The Two Noble Kinsmen* (New Brunswick, N.J., 1965) argues that the text derives from an exclusively Shakespearian original. Full-length works which include a consideration of the play include Charles Lamb's *Specimens of English Dramatic Poets* (1808); Ashley H. Thorndike's *The Influence of Beaumont and Fletcher on Shakespere* (1901; reprinted, New York, 1965); A.C. Bradley's *A Miscellany* (1929); Una Ellis-Fermor's *Shakespeare the Dramatist* (London: Methuen, 1961); Frank Kermode's *William Shakespeare: the Final Plays* (London: Longmans, 1963); and David L. Frost's *The School of Shakespeare* (Cambridge, 1968). Richard Proudfoot's essay 'Shakespeare and the New Dramatists of the King's Men' is included in *Later Shakespeare*, Stratford-upon-Avon Studies No.8 (London: Arnold, 1966). Periodical essays include Marco Mincoff's 'The Authorship of *The Two Noble Kinsmen*' in *English Studies*, XXXIII (1952); Theodore Spencer's '*The Two Noble Kinsmen*', in *Modern Philology*, XXVI (1939); and Philip Edwards's 'On the Design of *The Two Noble Kinsmen*', in *Review of English Literature*, V (1964). The last two essays are reprinted in the Signet edition of the play, edited by Clifford Leech.

# THE TWO NOBLE KINSMEN

## A tragi-comedy

WILLIAM SHAKESPEARE and
JOHN FLETCHER

## Characters

THESEUS, *Duke of Athens*
HIPPOLYTA, *Queen of the Amazons, and then wife of Theseus*
EMILIA, *her sister*
PIRITHOUS, *friend of Theseus*

PALAMON
ARCITE     *the two noble kinsmen, cousins from Thebes*

HYMEN, *god of marriage*
A BOY
ARTESIUS, *an Athenian soldier*
THREE QUEENS, *widows of kings killed in the siege of Thebes*

VALERIUS, *a Theban*

A HERALD
WOMAN, *servant of Emilia*
A GENTLEMAN
MESSENGERS
SIX KNIGHTS, *assisting Palamon and Arcite*
A SERVANT

GAOLER, *in charge of Theseus's prison*
DAUGHTER *of Gaoler*
WOOER *of Gaoler's Daughter*
TWO FRIENDS *of Gaoler*

BROTHER *of Gaoler*
A DOCTOR

SIX COUNTRYMEN, *one dressed as a bavian or baboon*
A SCHOOLMASTER
NELL *and four other* COUNTRY WENCHES
A TABORER

SPEAKER *of the Prologue and Epilogue*

*Nymphs, attendants, countrymen, garland-bearer, hunters, maids, executioner, guard of soldiers*

## The Text

The text used and reproduced here in full is taken from the edition prepared by N.W.Bawcutt for the New Penguin Shakespeare (Harmondsworth, 1977). The cuts made in the RSC version are indicated by square brackets in the text. The alterations and additions are indicated at the end of the text.

## PROLOGUE

*Flourish.*

> New plays and maidenheads are near akin,
> Much followed both, for both much money gi'en,
> If they stand sound and well. And a good play –
> Whose modest scenes blush on his marriage day,
> And shake to lose his honour – is like her
> That after holy tie and first night's stir
> Yet still is modesty, and still retains
> More of the maid to sight than husband's pains.
> We pray our play may be so; for I am sure
> It has a noble breeder, and a pure,
> A learnèd, and a poet never went
> More famous yet 'twixt Po and silver Trent.
> Chaucer, of all admired, the story gives;
> There constant to eternity it lives.
> If we let fall the nobleness of this,
> And the first sound this child hear be a hiss,
> How will it shake the bones of that good man,
> And make him cry from under ground 'O, fan
> From me the witless chaff of such a writer
> That blasts my bays and my famed works makes lighter
> Than Robin Hood!' This is the fear we bring;
> For, to say truth, it were an endless thing,
> And too ambitious, to aspire to him.
> Weak as we are, and almost breathless swim
> In this deep water, do but you hold out
> Your helping hands, and we shall tack about,
> And something do to save us; you shall hear
> Scenes, though below his art, may yet appear
> Worth two hours' travail. To his bones sweet sleep;
> Content to you. If this play do not keep
> A little dull time from us, we perceive
> Our losses fall so thick we must need leave.

*Flourish. Exit.*

## ACT ONE

### Scene One

*Music. Enter Hymen with a torch burning; a boy in a white robe before, singing and strewing flowers; after Hymen, a nymph, encompassed in her tresses, bearing a wheaten garland; then Theseus between two other nymphs with wheaten chaplets on their heads; then Hippolyta the bride, led by Pirithous, and another holding a garland over her head, her tresses likewise hanging; after her, Emilia holding up her train; then Artesius and attendants*

BOY (*sings*).
> Roses, their sharp spines being gone,
> Not royal in their smells alone,
>     But in their hue,
> Maiden pinks, of odour faint,
> Daisies smell-less, yet most quaint,
>     And sweet thyme true,
>
> Primrose, first-born child of Ver,
> Merry springtime's harbinger,
>     With harebells dim,
> Oxlips, in their cradles growing,
> Marigolds, on death-beds blowing,
>     Lark's-heels trim,
>
> All dear Nature's children sweet
> Lie 'fore bride and bridegroom's feet,
>     Blessing their sense.

*He strews flowers.*

> Not an angel of the air,
> Bird melodious or bird fair,
>     Is absent hence;
>
> The crow, the slanderous cuckoo, nor
> The boding raven, nor chough hoar,
>     Nor chattering pie,
> May on our bridehouse perch or sing,
> Or with them any discord bring,
>     But from it fly.

*Enter three Queens in black, with veils stained, with imperial crowns. The First Queen falls down at the foot of Theseus; the Second falls down at the foot of Hippolyta; the Third before Emilia*

FIRST QUEEN.
> For pity's sake and true gentility's,
> Hear and respect me!

SECOND QUEEN.                For your mother's sake,
And as you wish your womb may thrive with fair ones
Hear and respect me!

THIRD QUEEN.
Now for the love of him whom Jove hath marked
The honour of your bed, and for the sake
Of clear virginity, be advocate
For us and our distresses! This good deed
Shall raze you out o'th'book of trespasses
All you are set down there.

THESEUS.
Sad lady, rise.

HIPPOLYTA.            Stand up.

EMILIA.                        No knees to me.
What woman I may stead that is distressed
Does bind me to her.

THESEUS.
What's your request? Deliver you for all.

FIRST QUEEN.
We are three queens, whose sovereigns fell before
The wrath of cruel Creon; who endured
The beaks of ravens, talons of the kites,
And pecks of crows in the foul fields of Thebes.
He will not suffer us to burn their bones,
To urn their ashes, [nor to take th'offence
Of mortal loathsomeness from the blest eye
Of holy Phoebus,] but infects the winds
With stench of our slain lords. [1][O, pity, Duke!]
Thou purger of the earth, draw thy feared sword
That does good turns to th'world; give us the bones
Of our dead kings, that we may chapel them;
And of thy boundless goodness take some note
That for our crownèd heads we have no roof,
Save this which is the lion's and the bear's,
And vault to everything.

THESEUS.                    Pray you kneel not;
I was transported with your speech, and suffered
Your knees to wrong themselves. I have heard the fortunes
Of your dead lords, which gives me such lamenting
As wakes my vengeance and revenge for 'em.
King Capaneus was your lord; the day
That he should marry you, at such a season
As now it is with me, I met your groom.
By Mars's altar, you were that time fair;
Not Juno's mantle fairer than your tresses,

[Nor in more bounty spread her; your wheaten wreath
Was then nor threshed nor blasted; Fortune at you
Dimpled her cheeks with smiles. Hercules our kinsman –
Then weaker than your eyes – laid by his club;
He tumbled down upon his Nemean hide
And swore his sinews thawed.] O grief and time,
Fearful consumers, you will all devour!

FIRST QUEEN.
O, I hope some god,
Some god hath put his mercy in your manhood,
Whereto he'll infuse power, and press you forth
Our undertaker.

THESEUS.                [O, no knees, none, widow;
Unto the helmeted Bellona use them,
And][2] pray for me, your soldier; troubled I am.

*He turns away.*

SECOND QUEEN.
Honoured Hippolyta,
[Most dreaded Amazonian, that hast slain
The scythe-tusked boar, that with thy arm as strong
As it is white wast near to make the male
To thy sex captive, but that this thy lord,
Born to uphold creation in that honour
First Nature styled it in, shrunk thee into
The bound thou wast o'erflowing, at once subduing
Thy force and thy affection;] soldieress[3],
That equally canst poise sternness with pity,
[Whom now I know hast much more power on him
Than ever he had on thee, who owest his strength
And his love too, who is a servant for
The tenor of thy speech; dear glass of ladies,]
Bid him that we whom flaming war doth scorch
Under the shadow of his sword may cool us;
Require him he advance it o'er our heads;
Speak't in a woman's key, like such a woman
As any of us three; weep ere you fail.
Lend us a knee;
But touch the ground for us no longer time
Than a dove's motion when the head's plucked off;
Tell him, if he i'th'blood-sized field lay swollen,
Showing the sun his teeth, grinning at the moon,
What you would do.

HIPPOLYTA.                Poor lady, say no more;
I had as lief trace this good action with you
As that whereto I am going, and never yet
Went I so willing way. My lord is taken

Heart-deep with your distress; let him consider.
I'll speak anon.

THIRD QUEEN (*to Emilia*).                O, my petition was
Set down in ice, which by hot grief uncandied
Melts into drops; so sorrow wanting form
Is pressed with deeper matter.

EMILIA.                Pray stand up;
Your grief is written in your cheek.

THIRD QUEEN.                O woe,
You cannot read it there; there through my tears,
Like wrinkled pebbles in a glassy stream,
You may behold 'em. Lady, lady, alack,
He that will all the treasure know o'th'earth
Must know the centre too; he that will fish
For my least minnow, let him lead his line
To catch one at my heart. O, pardon me!
Extremity that sharpens sundry wits
Makes me a fool.

EMILIA.                Pray you say nothing, pray you;
Who cannot feel nor see the rain, being in't,
Knows neither wet nor dry. If that you were
The ground-piece of some painter, I would buy you
T'instruct me 'gainst a capital grief, indeed
Such heart-pierced demonstration; but alas,
Being a natural sister of our sex,
Your sorrow beats so ardently upon me
That it shall make a counter-reflect 'gainst
My brother's heart, and warm it to some pity
[Though it were made of stone. Pray have good comfort.]

THESEUS.
Forward to th'temple! Leave not out a jot
O'th'sacred ceremony.

FIRST QUEEN.                O, this celebration
Will longer last and be more costly than
Your suppliants' war. Remember that your fame
Knolls in the ear o'th'world; what you do quickly
Is not done rashly; [your first thought is more
Than others' laboured meditance, your premeditating
More than their actions.] But O Jove, your actions,
Soon as they move, as ospreys do the fish,
Subdue before they touch. Think, dear [4][Duke,] think
What beds our slain kings have.

SECOND QUEEN.                What grief our beds,
That our dear lords have none.

THIRD QUEEN.                None fit for th'dead.
Those that with cords, knives, drams, precipitance,
Weary of this world's light, have to themselves
Been death's most horrid agents, human grace
Affords them dust and shadow.

FIRST QUEEN.                But our lords
Lie blistering 'fore the visitating sun,
And were good kings when living.

THESEUS.                It is true,
And I will give you comfort,
To give your dead lords graves; the which to do
Must make some work with Creon.

[ FIRST QUEEN.                And that work
Presents itself to th'doing.
Now 'twill take form; the heats are gone tomorrow.
Then, bootless toil must recompense itself
With its own sweat; now, he's secure,
Not dreams we stand before your puissance,
Rinsing our holy begging in our eyes
To make petition clear.

SECOND QUEEN.                Now you may take him,
Drunk with his victory.

THIRD QUEEN.                And his army full
Of bread and sloth.

THESEUS.]                Artesius, [that best knowest
How to] draw out fit to this enterprise
[The primest for this proceeding, and] the number
To carry such a business, forth and levy
Our worthiest instruments, whilst we dispatch
This grand act of our life, this daring deed
Of fate in wedlock.

FIRST QUEEN.                [5][Dowagers,] take hands.
Let us be widows to our woes; delay
Commends us to a famishing hope.

ALL QUEENS.                Farewell.

[ SECOND QUEEN.
We come unseasonably; but when could grief
Cull forth, as unpanged judgement can, fittest time
For best solicitation?]

THESEUS.                Why, good ladies,
This is a service, whereto I am going,
Greater than any war; it more imports me
Than all the actions that I have foregone
Or futurely can cope.

FIRST QUEEN.                    The more proclaiming
Our suit shall be neglected, when her arms,
Able to lock Jove from a synod, shall
By warranting moonlight corslet thee; O, when
Her twinning cherries shall their sweetness fall
Upon thy tasteful lips, what wilt thou think
Of rotten kings or blubbered queens, what care
For what thou feelest not, what thou feelest being able
To make Mars spurn his drum? O, if thou couch
But one night with her, every hour in't will
Take hostage of thee for a hundred, and
Thou shalt remember nothing more than what
That banquet bids thee to.

HIPPOLYTA (*kneels*).               Though much unlike
You should be so transported, as much sorry
I should be such a suitor, yet I think
Did I not by th'abstaining of my joy,
Which breeds a deeper longing, cure their surfeit
That craves a present medicine, I should pluck
All ladies' scandal on me. Therefore, sir,
[As I shall here make trial of my prayers,
Either presuming them to have some force
Or sentencing for aye their vigour dumb,]
Prorogue this business we are going about, and hang
Your shield afore your heart, about that neck
Which is my fee, and which I freely lend
To do these poor queens service.

ALL QUEENS (*to Emilia*).               O, help now!
Our cause cries for your knee.

EMILIA (*kneels*).               If you grant not
My sister her petition in that force,
With that celerity and nature which
She makes it in, from henceforth I'll not dare
To ask you anything, nor be so hardy
Ever to take a husband.

THESEUS.               Pray stand up.
I am entreating of myself to do
That which you kneel to have me.

*All the ladies rise.*

                    Pirithous,
Lead on the bride; get you and pray the gods
For success and return; omit not anything
In the pretended celebration. Queens,
Follow your soldier. (*To Artesius:*) As before, hence you,
[And at the banks of Aulis] meet us with
The forces you can raise, [where we shall find

The moiety of a number for a business
More bigger-looked.] (*To Hippolyta:*) Since that our theme is
    haste,
I stamp this kiss upon thy current lip;

*He kisses her.*

Sweet, keep it as my token. – Set you forward,
For I will see you gone.

*The marriage procession moves towards the temple.*

Farewell, my beauteous sister, Pirithous,
Keep the feast full, bate not an hour on't.

PIRITHOUS.                    Sir,
I'll follow you at heels; the feast's solemnity
Shall want till your return.

THESEUS.               Cousin, I charge you,
Budge not from Athens. We shall be returning
Ere you can end this feast, of which I pray you
Make no abatement. Once more, farewell all.

*The procession goes out.*

FIRST QUEEN.
Thus dost thou still make good the tongue o'th'world.

SECOND QUEEN.
And earn'st a deity equal with Mars.

THIRD QUEEN.
If not above him, for
Thou being but mortal makest affections bend
To godlike honours; they themselves, some say,
Groan under such a mastery.

THESEUS.                    As we are men,
Thus should we do; being sensually subdued,
We lose our human title. Good cheer, ladies;
Now turn we towards your comforts.

*Flourish. Exeunt*

## Scene Two

*Enter Palamon and Arcite.*

ARCITE.
Dear Palamon, dearer in love than blood
And our prime cousin, yet unhardened in
The crimes of nature, let us leave the city

Thebes, and the temptings in't, before we further
Sully our gloss of youth;
[And here to keep in abstinence we shame
As in incontinence;] for not to swim
I'th'aid o'th'current were almost to sink,
At least to frustrate striving; and to follow
The common stream, 'twould bring us to an eddy
Where we should turn or drown; [if labour through,
Our gain but life and weakness.]

PALAMON.                                    [Your advice
Is cried up with example.] What strange ruins,
Since first we went to school, may we perceive
Walking in Thebes? Scars and bare weeds
The gain o'th'martialist, who did propound
To his bold ends honour and golden ingots,
Which though he won he had not, [and now flirted
By peace for whom he fought; who then shall offer
To Mars's so scorned altar?] I do bleed
When such I meet, and wish great Juno would
Resume her ancient fit of jealousy
To get the soldier work, that peace might purge
For her repletion, and retain anew
Her charitable heart, now hard and harsher
Than strife or war could be.

ARCITE.                                    Are you not out?
Meet you no ruin but the soldier in
The cranks and turns of Thebes? You did begin
As if you met decays of many kinds;
Perceive you none that do arouse your pity
But th'unconsidered soldier?

PALAMON.                                    Yes, I pity
Decays where'er I find them, [but such most
That sweating in an honourable toil
Are paid with ice to cool 'em.]

ARCITE.                                    'Tis not this
I did begin to speak of; this is virtue,
Of no respect in Thebes. I spake of Thebes,
How dangerous, if we will keep our honours,
It is for our residing, where every evil
Hath a good colour; where every seeming good's
A certain evil; [where not to be even jump
As they are, here were to be strangers, and
Such things to be, mere monsters.]

PALAMON.                                    ['Tis in our power –
Unless we fear that apes can tutor's – to
Be masters of our manners. What need I

Affect another's gait, which is not catching
Where there is faith, or to be fond upon
Another's way of speech, when by mine own
I may be reasonably conceived – saved too,
Speaking it truly? Why am I bound
By any generous bond to follow him
Follows his tailor, haply so long until
The followed make pursuit? Or let me know
Why mine own barber is unblest, with him
My poor chin too, for 'tis not scissored just
To such a favourite's glass? What canon is there
That does command my rapier from my hip
To dangle't in my hand, or to go tiptoe
Before the street be foul? Either I am
The fore-horse in the team, or I am none
That draw i'th'sequent trace.] These poor slight sores
Need not a plantain; that which rips my bosom
Almost to th'heart's –

ARCITE.                                    Our uncle Creon.

PALAMON.                                    He;
A most unbounded tyrant whose successes
[1][Makes] heaven unfeared, and villainy assured
Beyond its power there's nothing; almost puts
Faith in a fever, and deifies alone
Voluble chance; who only attributes
The faculties of [2][other] instruments
To his own nerves and act; commands [3][men] service,
And what they win in't, boot and glory; [one
That fears not to do harm; good, dares not.] Let
The blood of mine that's sib to him be sucked
From me with leeches! [Let them break and fall
Off me with that corruption.]

ARCITE.                                    Clear-spirited cousin,
Let's leave his court, that we may nothing share
Of his loud infamy; for our milk
Will relish of the pasture, and we must
Be vile or disobedient, not his kinsmen
In blood unless in quality.

PALAMON.                                    Nothing truer.
I think the echoes of his shames have deafed
The ears of heavenly justice; [widows' cries
Descend again into their throats, and have not
Due audience of the gods.]

*Enter Valerius.*

                                    Valerius.

VALERIUS.
      The King calls for you; yet be leaden-footed
      Till his great rage be off him. Phoebus, when
      He broke his whipstock and exclaimed against
      The horses of the sun, but whispered to
      The loudness of his fury.

PALAMON.                            Small winds shake him.
      But what's the matter?

VALERIUS.
      Theseus, who where he threats appals, hath sent
      Deadly defiance to him and pronounces
      Ruin to Thebes; [4][who] is at hand to seal
      The promise of his wrath.

ARCITE.                            Let him approach;
      But that we fear the gods in him, he brings not
      A jot of terror to us. Yet [5][what] man
      Thirds his own worth – [6][the case is each of ours] –
      When that his action's dregged with mind assured
      'Tis bad he goes about.

PALAMON.                            Leave that unreasoned;
      Our services stand now for Thebes, not Creon.
      [7][Yet] to be neutral to him were dishonour,
      Rebellious to oppose; therefore we must
      With him stand to the mercy of our fate,
      [Who hath bounded our last minute.]

ARCITE.                                  So we must.
      Is't said this war's afoot, or it shall be
      On fail of some condition?

VALERIUS.                        'Tis in motion;
      The intelligence of state came in the instant
      With the defier.

PALAMON.            Let's to the King, [who were he
      A quarter carrier of that honour which
      His enemy come in, the blood we venture
      Should be as for our health, which were not spent,
      Rather laid out for purchase. But alas,
      Our hands advanced before our hearts, what will
      The fall o'th'stroke do damage?

ARCITE.                            Let th'event,
      That never-erring arbitrator, tell us
      When we know all ourselves, and let us follow
      The becking of our chance.]

                                          *Exeunt.*

## Scene Three

*Enter Pirithous, Hippolyta and Emilia.*

PIRITHOUS.
      No further.

HIPPOLYTA.            Sir, farewell. Repeat my wishes
      To our great lord, of whose success I dare not
      Make any timorous question; [yet I wish him
      Excess and overflow of power, an't might be,
      To dure ill-dealing fortune.] Speed to him;
      Store never hurts good governors.

PIRITHOUS.                            Though I know
      His ocean needs not my poor drops, yet they
      Must yield their tribute there. (*To Emilia:*) My precious maid,
      Those best affections that the heavens infuse
      In their best-tempered pieces keep enthroned
      In your dear heart.

EMILIA.                  Thanks, sir. Remember me
      To our all-royal brother, [1][for whose speed
      The great Bellona I'll solicit; and
      Since in our terrene state petitions are not
      Without gifts understood, I'll offer to her
      What I shall be advised she likes. Our hearts]
      Are in his army, in his tent.

HIPPOLYTA.                        In's bosom.
      We have been soldiers, and we cannot weep
      When our friends don their helms, or put to sea,
      Or tell of babes broached on the lance, or women
      That have sod their infants in – and after ate them –
      The brine they wept at killing 'em; then if
      You stay to see of us such spinsters, we
      Should hold you here for ever.

PIRITHOUS.                        Peace be to you
      As I pursue this war, which shall be then
      Beyond further requiring.

                                          *Exit.*

EMILIA.                  [2][How his longing
      Follows his friend! Since his depart, his sports,
      Though craving seriousness and skill, passed slightly
      His careless execution, where nor gain
      Made him regard or loss consider, but
      Playing one business in his hand, another
      Directing in his head – his mind nurse equal
      To these so differing twins. Have you observed him
      Since our great lord departed?

HIPPOLYTA.                              With much labour;
    And I did love him for't. They two have cabined
    In many as dangerous as poor a corner,
    Peril and want contending; they have skiffed
    Torrents whose roaring tyranny and power
    I'th'least of these was dreadful; and they have
    Fought out together where death's self was lodged;
    Yet fate hath brought them off. Their knot of love,
    Tied, weaved, entangled, with so true, so long,
    And with a finger of so deep a cunning,
    May be outworn, never undone.] I think
    Theseus cannot be umpire to himself,
    Cleaving his conscience into twain and doing
    Each side like justice, which he loves best.

EMILIA.                                  Doubtless
    There is a best, and reason has no manners
    To say it is not you. I was acquainted
    Once with a time when I enjoyed a playfellow.
    You were at wars when she the grave enriched
    Who made too proud the bed; [took leave o'th'moon –
    Which then looked pale at parting –] when our count[3]
    Was each eleven.

HIPPOLYTA.          'Twas Flavina.

EMILIA.                          Yes.
    You talk of Pirithous' and Theseus' love;
    Theirs has more ground, is more maturely seasoned,
    More buckled with strong judgement, and their needs
    The one of th'other may be said to water
    Their intertangled roots of love. But I
    And she I sigh and spoke of were things innocent,
    Loved for we did, and like the elements
    That know not what, nor why, yet do effect
    Rare issues by their operance, our souls
    Did so to one another. What she liked
    Was then of me approved, what not, condemned,
    No more arraignment; the flower that I would pluck
    And put between my breasts – O, then but beginning
    To swell about the blossom – she would long
    Till she had such another, and commit it
    To the like innocent cradle, where phoenix-like
    They died in perfume; on my head no toy
    But was her pattern; [her affections – pretty,
    Though happily her careless wear – I followed
    For my most serious decking; had mine ear
    Stolen some new air, or at adventure hummed one
    From musical coinage, why, it was a note
    Whereon her spirits would sojourn – rather dwell on –

And sing it in her slumbers.] This[4] [rehearsal –
    Which every innocent wots well comes in
    Like old emportment's bastard –] has this end,
    That the true love 'tween maid and maid may be
    More than in sex dividual.

HIPPOLYTA.                  You're out of breath,
    And this high-speeded pace is but to say
    That you shall never – like the maid Flavina –
    Love any that's called man.

EMILIA.                      I am sure I shall not.

HIPPOLYTA.
    Now alack, weak sister,
    I must no more believe thee in this point,
    Though in't I know thou dost believe thyself,
    Than I will trust a sickly appetite
    That loathes even as it longs. But sure, my sister,
    If I were ripe for your persuasion, you
    Have said enough to shake me from the arm
    Of the all-noble Theseus, for whose fortunes
    I will now in and kneel, with great assurance
    That we, more than his Pirithous, possess
    The high throne in his heart.

EMILIA.                      I am not
    Against your faith, yet I continue mine.

                                        *Exeunt.*


## Scene Four

*Cornets. A battle struck within; then a retreat. Flourish. Then enter
Theseus, victor, with[1] Herald and attendants, and Palamon and Arcite
brought in on hearses. The three Queens meet him, and fall on their faces
before him.*

FIRST QUEEN.
    To thee no star be dark.

SECOND QUEEN.                Both heaven and earth
    Friend thee for ever.

THIRD QUEEN.            All the good that may
    Be wished upon thy head, I cry amen to't.

THESEUS.
    Th'impartial gods, who from the mounted heavens
    View us their mortal herd, behold who err,
    And in their time chastise. Go and find out
    The bones of your dead lords, and honour them

With treble ceremony; rather than a gap
Should be in their dear rites, we would supply't.
[2][But those we will depute which shall invest
You in your dignities, and even each thing
Our haste does leave imperfect. So adieu,
And]  heaven's good eyes look on you.

*Exeunt Queens with attendants.*

What are those?

[3][HERALD.
    Men of great quality, as may be judged
    By their appointment; some of Thebes have told's
    They are sisters' children, nephews to the King.

THESEUS.
    By th'helm of Mars, I saw them in the war,
    Like to a pair of lions, smeared with prey,
    Make lanes in troops aghast. I fixed my note
    Constantly on them, for they were a mark
    Worth a god's view. What prisoner was't that told me
    When I inquired their names?

HERALD.                         Wi'leave, they're called
    Arcite and Palamon.

THESEUS.                    'Tis right; those, those.]
    They are not dead?

HERALD.
    Nor in a state of life; had they been taken
    When their last hurts were given, 'twas possible
    They might have been recovered. Yet they breathe,
    And have the name of men.

THESEUS.                        [4][Then like men use 'em.
    The very lees of such, millions of rates,
    Exceed the wine of others.] All our surgeons
    Convent in their behoof; our richest balms,
    Rather than niggard, waste; their lives concern us
    Much more than Thebes is worth. [Rather than have 'em
    Freed of this plight and in their morning state,
    Sound and at liberty, I would 'em dead;
    But forty-thousandfold we had rather have 'em
    Prisoners to us than death.] Bear 'em [5][speedily
    From our kind air, to them unkind], and minister
    What man to man may do [– for our sake, more,
    Since I have known frights, fury, friends' behests,
    Love's provocations, zeal, a mistress' task,
    Desire of liberty, a fever, madness,
    Hath set a mark which nature could not reach to
    Without some imposition, sickness in will

O'er-wrestling strength in reason. For our love
And great Apollo's mercy, all our best
Their best skill tender]. Lead into the city,
Where having bound things scattered, we will post
To Athens 'fore our army.

*Flourish. Exeunt.*

## Scene Five

*Music. Enter the Queens with the hearses of their knights, in a funeral
solemnity, with attendants.*

> *Song*
> Urns and odours bring away;
> Vapours, sighs, darken the day;
>     Our dole more deadly looks than dying;
> Balms and gums and heavy cheers,
> Sacred vials filled with tears,
>     And clamours through the wild air flying.
> Come all sad and solemn shows
> That are quick-eyed pleasure's foes;
> We convent naught else but woes,
> We convent naught else but woes.

[THIRD QUEEN.
    This funeral path brings to your household's grave.
    Joy seize on you again; peace sleep with him.

SECOND QUEEN.
    And this to yours.

FIRST QUEEN.             Yours this way. Heavens lend
    A thousand differing ways to one sure end.]

THIRD QUEEN.
    This world's a city full of straying streets,
    And death's the market-place, where each one meets.

*Exeunt severally.*

# ACT TWO

## Scene One

*Enter Gaoler and Wooer.*

GAOLER. I may depart with little while I live; something I may cast to you, not much. Alas, the prison I keep, though it be for great ones, yet they seldom come; before one salmon, you shall take a number of minnows. I am given out to be better lined [than it can appear to me report is a true speaker]. I would I were really that I am delivered to be. Marry, what I have, be it what it will, I will assure upon my daughter at the day of my death.

WOOER. Sir, I demand no more than your own offer, and I will estate your daughter in what I have promised.

GAOLER. [Well, we will talk more of this when the solemnity is past.] But have you a full promise of her? When that shall be seen, I tender my consent.

*Enter Gaoler's Daughter with rushes.*

WOOER. I have, sir. Here she comes.

GAOLER. Your friend and I have chanced to name you here, upon the old business; but no more of that now. So soon as the court hurry is over we will have an end of it. I'th'meantime look tenderly to the two prisoners; I can tell you they are princes.

DAUGHTER. These strewings are for their chamber. 'Tis pity they are in prison, and 'twere pity they should be out. I do think they have patience to make any adversity ashamed; the prison itself is proud of 'em, and they have all the world in their chamber.

GAOLER. They are famed to be a pair of absolute men.

DAUGHTER. By my troth, I think fame but stammers 'em; they stand a grece above the reach of report.]

GAOLER. I heard them reported in the battle to be the only doers.

DAUGHTER. [Nay, most likely, for they are noble sufferers.] I marvel how they would have looked had they been victors, [that with such a constant nobility enforce a freedom out of bondage,] making misery their mirth and affliction a toy to jest at.

GAOLER. Do they so?

DAUGHTER. It seems to me they have no more sense of their captivity than I of ruling Athens; they eat well, look merrily, discourse of many things, but nothing of their own restraint and disasters. [Yet sometime a divided sigh, martyred as 'twere i'th' deliverance, will break from one of them; when the other presently gives it so sweet a rebuke that I could wish myself a sigh to be so chid, or at least a sigher to be comforted.]

WOOER. I never saw 'em.

GAOLER. The Duke himself came privately in the night, and so did they; what the reason of it is I know not.

*Enter Palamon and Arcite above.*

Look, yonder they are; that's Arcite looks out.

DAUGHTER. No, sir, no, that's Palamon! Arcite is the lower of the twain; [you may perceive a part of him.]

GAOLER. Go to, leave your pointing. They would not make us their object. Out of their sight!

DAUGHTER. It is a holiday to look on them. Lord, the difference of men!

*Exeunt Gaoler, Daughter and Wooer.*

PALAMON.
How do you, noble cousin?

ARCITE. How do you, sir?

PALAMON.
Why, strong enough to laugh at misery,
And bear the chance of war; yet we are prisoners
I fear for ever, cousin.

ARCITE. I believe it,
And to that destiny have patiently
Laid up my hour to come.

PALAMON. O cousin Arcite,
Where is Thebes now? Where is our noble country?
Where are our friends and kindreds? Never more
Must we behold those comforts, never see
The hardy youths strive for the games of honour,
Hung with the painted favours of their ladies,
Like tall ships under sail; then start amongst 'em
And as an east wind leave 'em all behind us,
Like lazy clouds, whilst Palamon and Arcite,
Even in the wagging of a wanton leg,
Outstripped the people's praises, won the garlands,
Ere they have time to wish 'em ours. O, never
Shall we two exercise, like twins of honour,
Our arms again, and feel our fiery horses
Like proud seas under us! Our good swords now –
Better the red-eyed god of war ne'er wore –
Ravished our sides, like age must run to rust,
And deck the temples of those gods that hate us;

These hands shall never draw 'em out like lightning
To blast whole armies more.

ARCITE.                               No, Palamon,
Those hopes are prisoners with us; here we are,
And here the graces of our youths must wither
Like a too timely spring; here age must find us,
And – which is heaviest, Palamon – unmarried.
The sweet embraces of a loving wife,
Loaden with kisses, armed with thousand cupids,
Shall never clasp our necks; no issue know us;
No figures of ourselves shall we e'er see
To glad our age, and like young eagles teach 'em
Boldly to gaze against bright arms, and say
'Remember what your fathers were, and conquer!'
The fair-eyed maids shall weep our banishments,
And in their songs curse ever-blinded fortune,
Till she for shame see what a wrong she has done
To youth and nature. This is all our world;
We shall know nothing here but one another,
Hear nothing but the clock that tells our woes.
The vine shall grow, but we shall never see it;
Summer shall come, and with her all delights,
But dead-cold winter must inhabit here still.

PALAMON.
'Tis too true, Arcite. [To our Theban hounds,
That shook the agèd forest with their echoes,
No more now must we hallow, no more shake
Our pointed javelins, whilst the angry swine
Flies like a Parthian quiver from our rages,
Struck with our well-steeled darts.] All valiant uses,
The food and nourishment of noble minds,
In us two here shall perish; we shall die –
Which is the curse of honour – lastly,
Children of grief and ignorance.

ARCITE.                               Yet, cousin,
Even from the bottom of these miseries,
From all that fortune can inflict upon us,
I see two comforts rising, two mere blessings,
If the gods please; to hold here a brave patience,
And the enjoying of our griefs together.
Whilst Palamon is with me, let me perish
If I think this our prison.

PALAMON.               Certainly,
'Tis a main goodness, cousin, that our fortunes
Were twinned together. 'Tis most true, two souls
Put in two noble bodies, let 'em suffer
The gall of hazard, so they grow together,

Will never sink, they must not; say they could,
A willing man dies sleeping and all's done.

ARCITE.
Shall we make worthy uses of this place
That all men hate so much?

PALAMON.                     How, gentle cousin?

ARCITE.
Let's think this prison holy sanctuary,
To keep us from corruption of worse men.
We are young and yet desire the ways of honour,
That liberty and common conversation,
The poison of pure spirits, might like women
Woo us to wander from. What worthy blessing
[1][Can be] but our imaginations
May make it ours? And here being thus together,
We are an endless mine to one another;
We are one another's wife, ever begetting
New births of love; we are father, friends, acquaintance;
We are, in one another, families.
I am your heir, and you are mine; this place
Is our inheritance; no hard oppressor
Dare take this from us; here with a little patience
We shall live long and loving. No surfeits seek us;
The hand of war hurts none here, nor the seas
Swallow their youth. Were we at liberty,
A wife might part us lawfully, or business;
Quarrels consume us; envy of ill men
Crave our acquaintance. I might sicken, cousin,
Where you should never know it, and so perish
Without your noble hand to close mine eyes,
Or prayers to the gods; a thousand chances,
Were we from hence, would sever us.

PALAMON.                     You have made me –
I thank you, cousin Arcite – almost wanton
With my captivity. What a misery
It is to live abroad, and everywhere!
'Tis like a beast, methinks. I find the court here;
I am sure, a more content; and all those pleasures
That woo the wills of men to vanity
I see through now, and am sufficient
To tell the world 'tis but a gaudy shadow
That old Time as he passes by takes with him.
What had we been, old in the court of Creon,
Where sin is justice, lust and ignorance
The virtues of the great ones? Cousin Arcite,
Had not the loving gods found this place for us,
We had died as they do, ill old men, unwept,

And had their epitaphs, the people's curses.
Shall I say more?

ARCITE.                    I would hear you still.

PALAMON.                              Ye shall.
Is there record of any two that loved
Better than we do, Arcite?

ARCITE.              Sure there cannot.

PALAMON.
I do not think it possible our friendship
Should ever leave us.

ARCITE.                 Till our deaths it cannot;

*Enter Emilia and her Woman below.*

And after death our spirits shall be led
To those that love eternally.

*Palamon sees Emilia.*

                    Speak on, sir.

EMILIA.
This garden has a world of pleasures in't.
What flower is this?

WOMAN.            'Tis called narcissus, madam.

EMILIA.
That was a fair boy, certain, but a fool
To love himself; were there not maids enough?

ARCITE (*to Palamon*).
Pray, forward.

PALAMON.       Yes.

EMILIA (*to Woman*).    Or were they all hard-hearted?

WOMAN.
They could not be to one so fair.

EMILIA.                   Thou wouldst not.

WOMAN.
I think I should not, madam.

EMILIA.                   That's a good wench;
But take heed to your kindness, though.

WOMAN.                        Why, madam?

EMILIA.
Men are mad things.

ARCITE.            Will ye go forward, cousin?

EMILIA.
Canst not thou work such flowers in silk, wench?

WOMAN.                               Yes.

EMILIA.
I'll have a gown full of 'em and of these.
This is a pretty colour; will't not do
Rarely upon a skirt, wench?

WOMAN.                   Dainty, madam.

ARCITE.
Cousin, cousin, how do you, sir? Why, Palamon!

PALAMON.
Never till now I was in prison, Arcite.

ARCITE.
Why, what's the matter, man?

PALAMON.                   Behold, and wonder.
By heaven, she is a goddess.

ARCITE.               Ha!

PALAMON.               Do reverence;
She is a goddess, Arcite.

EMILIA.               Of all flowers
Methinks a rose is best.

WOMAN.               Why, gentle madam?

EMILIA.
It is the very emblem of a maid;
For when the west wind courts her gently,
How modestly she blows, and paints the sun
With her chaste blushes! When the north comes near her,
Rude and impatient, then, like chastity,
She locks her beauties in her bud again,
And leaves him to base briars.

WOMAN.                   Yet, good madam,
Sometimes her modesty will blow so far
She falls for't; a maid,
If she have any honour, would be loath
To take example by her.

EMILIA.               Thou art wanton.

ARCITE.
She is wondrous fair.

PALAMON.            She is all the beauty extant.

EMILIA.
The sun grows high, let's walk in. Keep these flowers;

We'll see how near art can come near their colours.
I am wondrous merry-hearted, I could laugh now.

WOMAN.
I could lie down, I am sure.

EMILIA.                              And take one with you?

WOMAN.
That's as we bargain, madam.

EMILIA.                         Well, agree then.

*Exeunt Emilia and Woman.*

PALAMON.
What think you of this beauty?

ARCITE.                              'Tis a rare one.

PALAMON.
Is't but a rare one?

ARCITE.             Yes, a matchless beauty.

PALAMON.
Might not a man well lose himself and love her?

ARCITE.
I cannot tell what you have done; I have,
Beshrew mine eyes for't! Now I feel my shackles.

PALAMON.
You love her, then?

ARCITE.             Who would not?

PALAMON.                         And desire her?

ARCITE.
Before my liberty.

PALAMON.
I saw her first.

ARCITE.           That's nothing.

PALAMON.                         But it shall be.

ARCITE.
I saw her too.

PALAMON.       Yes, but you must not love her.

ARCITE I will not, as you do, to worship her
As she is heavenly and a blessèd goddess.
I love her as a woman, to enjoy her;
So both may love.

PALAMON.           You shall not love at all.

ARCITE.
Not love at all? Who shall deny me?

PALAMON.
I that first saw her; I that took possession
First with mine eye of all those beauties
In her revealed to mankind. If thou lovest her,
Or entertainest a hope to blast my wishes,
Thou art a traitor, Arcite, and a fellow
False as thy title to her. Friendship, blood,
And all the ties between us I disclaim,
If thou once think upon her.

ARCITE.                       Yes, I love her,
And if the lives of all my name lay on it,
I must do so; I love her with my soul.
If that will lose ye, farewell, Palamon!
I say again
I love her, and in loving her maintain
I am as worthy and as free a lover,
And have as just a title to her beauty
As any Palamon or any living
That is a man's son.

PALAMON.           Have I called thee friend?

ARCITE.
Yes, and have found me so; why are you moved thus?
Let me deal coldly with you. Am not I
Part of your blood, part of your soul? You have told me
That I was Palamon and you were Arcite.

PALAMON.                                    Yes.

ARCITE.
Am not I liable to those affections,
Those joys, griefs, angers, fears, my friend shall suffer?

PALAMON.
Ye may be.

ARCITE.      Why then would you deal so cunningly,
So strangely, so unlike a noble kinsman,
To love alone? Speak truly, do you think me
Unworthy of her sight?

PALAMON.              No, but unjust,
If thou pursue that sight.

ARCITE.                    Because another
First sees the enemy, shall I stand still
And let mine honour down, and never charge?

PALAMON.
Yes, if he be but one.

ARCITE.                    But say that one
Had rather combat me?

PALAMON.                    Let that one say so,
And use thy freedom; else if thou pursuest her,
Be as that cursèd man that hates his country,
A branded villain.

ARCITE.                    You are mad.

PALAMON.                    I must be,
Till thou art worthy, Arcite; it concerns me,
And in this madness if I hazard thee
And take thy life, I deal but truly.

ARCITE.                    Fie, sir,
You play the child extremely. I will love her;
I must, I ought to do so, and I dare,
And all this justly.

PALAMON.            O that now, that now
Thy false self and thy friend had but this fortune
To be one hour at liberty, and grasp
Our good swords in our hands; I would quickly teach thee
What 'twere to filch affection from another!
Thou art baser in it than a cutpurse.
Put but thy head out of this window more,
And as I have a soul, I'll nail thy life to't.

ARCITE.
Thou darest not, fool, thou canst not, thou art feeble.
Put my head out? I'll throw my body out,
And leap the garden, when I see her next,
And pitch between her arms to anger thee.

*Enter Gaoler above.*

PALAMON.
No more; the keeper's coming. I shall live
To knock thy brains out with my shackles.

ARCITE.                    Do.

GAOLER.
By your leave, gentlemen.

PALAMON.                    Now, honest keeper?

GAOLER.
Lord Arcite, you must presently to th'Duke.
The cause I know not yet.

ARCITE.                    I am ready, keeper.

GAOLER.
Prince Palamon, I must awhile bereave you

Of your fair cousin's company.

*Exeunt Arcite and Gaoler.*

PALAMON.                    And me too,
Even when you please, of life. Why is he sent for?
It may be he shall marry her; he's goodly,
And like enough the Duke hath taken notice
Both of his blood and body. But his falsehood!
Why should a friend be so treacherous? If that
Get him a wife so noble and so fair,
Let honest men ne'er love again. Once more
I would but see this fair one; blessèd garden,
And fruit, and flowers more blessèd that still blossom
As her bright eyes shine on ye! Would I were
For all the fortune of my life hereafter
Yon little tree, yon blooming apricot;
How I would spread, and fling my wanton arms
In at her window! I would bring her fruit
Fit for the gods to feed on; youth and pleasure
Still as she tasted should be doubled on her,
And if she be not heavenly, I would make her
So near the gods in nature, they should fear her;
And then I am sure she would love me.

*Enter Gaoler.*

                        How now, keeper?
Where's Arcite?

GAOLER.            Banished. Prince Pirithous
Obtained his liberty; but never more,
Upon his oath and life, must he set foot
Upon this kingdom.

PALAMON.                    He's a blessèd man!
He shall see Thebes again, and call to arms
The bold young men, that when he bids 'em charge
Fall on like fire. Arcite shall have a fortune,
If he dare make himself a worthy lover,
[Yet in the field to strike a battle for her;
And if he lose her then, he's a cold coward.]
How bravely may he bear himself to win her
If he be noble Arcite; thousand ways!
Were I at liberty, I would do things
Of such a virtuous greatness that this lady,
This blushing virgin, should take manhood to her,
And seek to ravish me!

GAOLER.                    My lord, for you
I have this charge too –

PALAMON.                    To discharge my life?

GAOLER.
　No, but from this place to remove your lordship;
　The windows are too open.

PALAMON.　　　　　　　　Devils take 'em
　That are so envious to me! Prithee kill me.

GAOLER.
　And hang for't afterward?

PALAMON.　　　　　　By this good light,
　Had I a sword I would kill thee.

GAOLER.　　　　　　　　　Why, my lord?

PALAMON.
　Thou bringest such pelting scurvy news continually
　Thou art not worthy life. I will not go.

GAOLER.
　Indeed you must, my lord.

PALAMON.　　　　　　　May I see the garden.

GAOLER.
　No.

PALAMON. Then I am resolved, I will not go.

GAOLER.
　I must constrain you then; and for you are dangerous,
　I'll clap more irons on you.

PALAMON.　　　　　　Do, good keeper.
　I'll shake 'em so, ye shall not sleep;
　I'll make ye a new morris. Must I go?

GAOLER.
　There is no remedy.

PALAMON.　　　　　Farewell, kind window;
　May rude wind never hurt thee. O my lady,
　If ever thou hast felt what sorrow was,
　Dream how I suffer. – Come, now bury me.

　　　　　　　　　　　　　　　　　　　*Exeunt.*

## Scene Two

*Enter Arcite.*

ARCITE.
　Banished the kingdom? 'Tis a benefit,
　A mercy I must thank 'em for; but banished
　The free enjoying of that face I die for,
　O, 'twas a studied punishment, a death
　Beyond imagination; such a vengeance
　That, were I old and wicked, all my sins
　Could never pluck upon me. Palamon,
　Thou hast the start now; thou shalt stay and see
　Her bright eyes break each morning 'gainst thy window,
　And let in life into thee; [1][thou shalt feed
　Upon the sweetness of a noble beauty
　That Nature ne'er exceeded, nor ne'er shall.
　Good gods, what happiness has Palamon!
　Twenty to one, he'll come to] speak to her,
　And if she be as gentle as she's fair,
　I know she's his; he has a tongue will tame
　Tempests, and make the wild rocks wanton. Come what can
　　　come,
　The worst is death; I will not leave the kingdom.
　I know mine own is but a heap of ruins,
　And no redress there. If I go, he has her.
　I am resolved another shape shall make me,
　Or end my fortunes. Either way, I am happy;
　I'll see her and be near her, or no more.

*Enter four Country-people and one with a garland before them.*

2

FIRST COUNTRYMAN.
　My masters, I'll be there, that's certain.

SECOND COUNTRYMAN.
　And I'll be there.

[THIRD COUNTRYMAN.
　And I.]

FOURTH COUNTRYMAN.
　Why, then, have with ye, boys; 'tis but a chiding.
　Let the plough play today; I'll tickle't out
　Of the jades' tails tomorrow.

FIRST COUNTRYMAN.　　　　　　I am sure
　To have my wife as jealous as a turkey;
　But that's all one, I'll go through, let her mumble.

SECOND COUNTRYMAN.
　Clap her abroad tomorrow night and stow her,
　And all's made up again.

THIRD COUNTRYMAN.　　Ay, do but put
　A fescue in her fist, [and you shall see her
　Take a new lesson out, and be a good wench.
　Do we all hold against the maying?

FOURTH COUNTRYMAN.　　　　　　Hold?
　What should ail us?

THIRD COUNTRYMAN.    Arcas will be there.]

SECOND COUNTRYMAN.    [And Sennois
And Rycas, and three]  better lads ne'er danced
Under green tree; and ye know what wenches, ha!
But will the dainty dominie, the schoolmaster,
Keep touch, do you think? [For] he does all, ye know.

THIRD COUNTRYMAN.
He'll eat a hornbook ere he fail. Go to,
The matter's too far driven between him
And the [3][tanner's] daughter to let slip now;
[And she must see the Duke, and she must dance too.]

FOURTH COUNTRYMAN.
Shall we be lusty?

SECOND COUNTRYMAN. All the boys in Athens
Blow wind i'th'breech on's!

*He dances.*

                    And here I'll be
And there I'll be, for our town, and here again
And there again! Ha, boys, hey for the weavers!

FIRST COUNTRYMAN.
This must be done i'th'woods.

FOURTH COUNTRYMAN.         O, pardon me.

[SECOND COUNTRYMAN.
By any means, our thing of learning says so;
Where he himself will edify the Duke
Most parlously in our behalfs. He's excellent i'th'woods;
Bring him to th'plains, his learning makes no cry.]

THIRD COUNTRYMAN.
We'll see the sports, then every man to's tackle;
And, sweet companions, let's rehearse [by any means
Before the ladies see us, and do sweetly,
And God knows what may come on't].

FOURTH COUNTRYMAN.
Content; [the sports once ended, we'll perform.
Away, boys, and hold!]

ARCITE.              By your leaves, honest friends;
Pray you, whither go you?

FOURTH COUNTRYMAN.    Whither?
Why, what a question's that!

ARCITE.              Yes, 'tis a question
To me that know not.

THIRD COUNTRYMAN.    To the games, my friend.

SECOND COUNTRYMAN.
Where were you bred you know it not?

ARCITE.                    Not far, sir.
Are there such games today?

FIRST COUNTRYMAN.        Yes, marry are there,
And such as you never saw. The Duke himself
Will be in person there.

ARCITE.            What pastimes are they?

SECOND COUNTRYMAN.
Wrestling and running. (*Aside*.) 'Tis a pretty fellow.

THIRD COUNTRYMAN.
Thou wilt not go along?

ARCITE.            Not yet, sir.

FOURTH COUNTRYMAN.            Well, sir,
Take your own time. – Come, boys.

FIRST COUNTRYMAN.            My mind misgives me.
This fellow has a vengeance trick o'th'hip;
Mark how his body's made for't.

SECOND COUNTRYMAN.        I'll be hanged, though,
If he dare venture; hang him, plum porridge!
He wrestle? He roast eggs! Come, let's be gone, lads.

                    *Exeunt four Countrymen and garland-bearer.*

ARCITE.
This is an offered opportunity
I durst not wish for. [Well I could have wrestled,
The best men called it excellent; and run
Swifter than wind upon a field of corn,
Curling the wealthy ears, never flew.] I'll venture,
And in some poor disguise be there; who knows
Whether my brows may not be girt with garlands,
And happiness prefer me to a place
Where I may ever dwell in sight of her?

                                    *Exit.*

## Scene Three

*Enter Gaoler's Daughter alone.*

DAUGHTER.
Why should I love this gentleman? 'Tis odds

He never will affect me; I am base,
My father the mean keeper of his prison,
And he a prince. To marry him is hopeless;
To be his whore is witless. Out upon't!
What pushes are we wenches driven to
When fifteen once has found us! First I saw him;
I, seeing, thought he was a goodly man;
He has as much to please a woman in him –
If he please to bestow it so – as ever
These eyes yet looked on. Next, I pitied him,
And so would any young wench, o' my conscience,
That ever dreamed, or vowed her maidenhead
To a young handsome man. Then I loved him,
Extremely loved him, infinitely loved him;
And yet he had a cousin, fair as he too;
But in my heart was Palamon, [and there,
Lord, what a coil he keeps!] To hear him
Sing in an evening, what a heaven it is!
And yet his songs are sad ones. Fairer spoken
Was never gentleman; when I come in
To bring him water in a morning, first
He bows his noble body, then salutes me, thus:
'Fair, gentle maid, good morrow; may thy goodness
Get thee a happy husband.' Once he kissed me;
I loved my lips the better ten days after –
[Would he would do so every day! He grieves much,
And me as much to see his misery.]
What should I do to make him know I love him?
For I would fain enjoy him. Say I ventured
To set him free? What says the law then? Thus much
For law or kindred! I will do it;
And this night, or tomorrow, he shall love me.

*Exit.*

## Scene Four

*A short flourish of cornets, and shouts within. Enter Theseus, Hippolyta, Pirithous, Emilia, Arcite as a countryman, with a garland, and other countrymen and attendants.*

THESEUS (*to Arcite*).
You have done worthily; I have not seen,
Since Hercules, a man of tougher sinews.
Whate'er you are, you run the best and wrestle
That these times can allow.

ARCITE.                          I am proud to please you.

THESEUS.
What country bred you?

ARCITE.                          This; but far off, prince.

THESEUS.
Are you a gentleman?

ARCITE.                          My father said so,
And to those gentle uses gave me life.

[THESEUS.
Are you his heir?

ARCITE.                          His youngest, sir.

THESEUS.                                    Your father
Sure is a happy sire, then. What proves you?

ARCITE.
A little of all noble qualities;]
I could have kept a hawk, and well have hallowed
To a deep cry of dogs; I dare not praise
My feat in horsemanship, yet they that knew me
Would say it was my best piece; last, and greatest,
I would be thought a soldier.

THESEUS.                          You are perfect.

PIRITHOUS.
Upon my soul, a proper man.

EMILIA.                          He is so.

PIRITHOUS.
How do you like him, lady?

HIPPOLYTA.                          I admire him;
[I have not seen so young a man so noble –
If he say true – of his sort.]

EMILIA.                          [Believe]
His mother was a wondrous handsome woman;
His face methinks goes that way.

HIPPOLYTA.                          But his body
And fiery mind illustrate a brave father.

PIRITHOUS.
Mark how his virtue, like a hidden sun,
Breaks through his baser garments.

HIPPOLYTA.                          He's well got, sure.

THESEUS.
What made you seek this place, sir?

ARCITE.                          Noble Theseus,

To purchase name, and do my ablest service
[To such a well-found wonder as thy worth;]
For only in thy court, of all the world,
Dwells fair-eyed honour.

PIRITHOUS.                        All his words are worthy.

THESEUS.
Sir, we are much indebted to your travel,
Nor shall you lose your wish; Pirithous,
Dispose of this fair gentleman.

PIRITHOUS.                    Thanks, Theseus.
(*To Arcite:*)
Whate'er you are you're mine, and I shall give you
To a most noble service, to this lady,
This bright young virgin; pray observe her goodness.
You have honoured her fair birthday with your virtues,
And as your due, you're hers; kiss her fair hand, sir.

ARCITE.
Sir, you're a noble giver. (*To Emilia:*) Dearest beauty,
Thus let me seal my vowed faith.

*He kisses her hand.*

                              When your servant,
Your most unworthy creature, but offends you,
Command him die; he shall.

EMILIA.                        That were too cruel.
If you deserve well, sir, I shall soon see't.
You're mine;
And somewhat better than your rank I'll use you.

PIRITHOUS.
I'll see you furnished, and because you say
You are a horseman, I must needs entreat you
This afternoon to ride; but 'tis a rough one.

ARCITE.
I like him better, prince; I shall not then
Freeze in my saddle.

THESEUS (*to Hippolyta*).    Sweet, you must be ready,
And you, Emilia, and you, friend, and all,
Tomorrow by the sun, to do observance
To flowery May, in Dian's wood. Wait well, sir,
Upon your mistress; Emily, I hope
He shall not go afoot.

EMILIA.                    That were a shame, sir.
While I have horses. (*To Arcite:*) Take your choice, and what
You want at any time, let me but know it;

If you serve faithfully, I dare assure you
You'll find a loving mistress.

[ARCITE.                        If I do not,
Let me find that my father ever hated,
Disgrace and blows.]

THESEUS.                    Go lead the way; you have won it.
It shall be so; you shall receive all dues
Fit for the honour you have won, 'twere wrong else. –
Sister, beshrew my heart, you have a servant
That, if I were a woman, would be master;
But you are wise.

EMILIA.              I hope, too wise for that, sir.

*Flourish: Exeunt.*

## Scene Five

*Enter Gaoler's Daughter alone.*

DAUGHTER.
Let all the dukes and all the devils roar;
He is at liberty. [I have ventured for him,
And out I have brought him.] To a little wood
A mile hence I have sent him, [where a cedar
Higher than all the rest spreads like a plane,
Fast by a brook,] and there he shall keep close,
Till I provide him files and food, for yet
His iron bracelets are not off. O love,
What a stout-hearted child thou art! My father
Durst better have endured cold iron than done it.
I love him beyond love, and beyond reason,
Or wit, or safety; I have made him know it.
I care not, I am desperate. If the law
Find me, and then condemn me for't, some wenches,
Some honest-hearted maids, will sing my dirge,
And tell to memory my death was noble,
Dying almost a martyr. That way he takes
I purpose is my way too; sure he cannot
Be so unmanly as to leave me here?
[If he do, maids will not so easily
Trust men again.] And yet he has not thanked me
For what I have done, no, not so much as kissed me,
And that, methinks, is not [1][so well; nor scarcely
Could I persuade him to become a free man,
He made such scruples of the wrong he did
To me and to my father.] Yet I hope,
When he considers more, this love of mine

Will take more root within him. Let him do
What he will with me, so he use me kindly;
For use me so he shall, [or I'll proclaim him,
And to his face, no man.] I'll presently
Provide him necessaries, and pack my clothes up,
And where there is a path of ground I'll venture,
So he be with me; by him, like a shadow,
I'll ever dwell. Within this hour the hubbub
Will be all o'er the prison; I am then
Kissing the man they look for. Farewell, father;
[Get many more such prisoners, and such daughters,
And shortly you may keep yourself.] Now to him.

*Exit.*

## ACT THREE

### Scene One

*Cornets in sundry places. Noise and hallowing as of people a-maying. Enter Arcite alone.*

ARCITE.
The Duke has lost Hippolyta; each took
A several laund. This is a solemn rite
They owe bloomed May, and the Athenians pay it
To th'heart of ceremony. O queen Emilia,
Fresher than May, sweeter
Than her gold buttons on the boughs, [or all
Th'enamelled knacks o'th'mead or garden – yea,
We challenge too the bank of any nymph
That makes the stream seem flowers – thou,] O jewel
O'th'wood, o'th'world, [1][hast] likewise blessed a place
With thy sole presence. [In thy rumination
That I, poor man, might eftsoons come between
And chop on some cold thought!] Thrice blessèd chance
To drop on such a mistress, expectation
Most guiltless on't! [Tell me, O Lady Fortune,
Next after Emily my sovereign, how far
I may be proud.] She takes strong note of me,
Hath made me near her; and this beauteous morn,
The primest of all the year, presents me with
A brace of horses; [two such steeds might well
Be by a pair of kings backed, in a field
That their crowns' titles tried. Alas, alas,]
Poor cousin Palamon, poor prisoner, [thou
So little dreamest upon my fortune that
Thou thinkest thyself the happier thing, to be
So near Emilia; me thou deemest at Thebes,
And therein wretched, although free. But] if
Thou knewest my mistress breathed on me, and that
I eared her language, lived in her eye – O coz,
What passion would enclose thee!

*Enter Palamon as out of a bush, with his shackles; he bends his fist at Arcite.*

PALAMON.                                    Traitor kinsman,
Thou shouldst perceive my passion, if these signs
Of prisonment were off me, and this hand
But owner of a sword. By all oaths in one,
I and the justice of my love would make thee
A confessed traitor, O thou most perfidious
That ever gently looked, the voidest of honour

That e'er bore gentle token, falsest cousin
That ever blood made kin. Callest thou her thine?
I'll prove it in my shackles, with these hands,
Void of appointment, that thou liest, and art
A very thief in love, [a chaffy lord
Not worth the name of villain. Had I a sword,
And these house-clogs away] –

ARCITE.                                    Dear cousin Palamon –

PALAMON.
Cozener Arcite, [give me language such
As thou hast showed me feat.]

ARCITE.                                    Not finding in
The circuit of my breast any gross stuff
To form me like your blazon holds me to
This gentleness of answer: 'tis your passion
That thus mistakes, the which to you being enemy
Cannot to me be kind. Honour and honesty
I cherish and depend on, howsoe'er
You skip them in me, and with them, fair coz,
I'll maintain my proceedings. Pray be pleased
To show in generous terms your griefs, since that
Your question's with your equal, who professes
To clear his own way with the mind and sword
Of a true gentleman.

PALAMON.                    That thou durst, Arcite!

ARCITE.
My coz, my coz, you have been well advertised
How much I dare; you've seen me use my sword
Against th'advice of fear. Sure of another
You would not hear me doubted, but your silence
Should break out, though i'th'sanctuary.

PALAMON.                                    Sir,
I have seen you move in such a place which well
Might justify your manhood; you were called
A good knight and a bold. But the whole week's not fair
If any day it rain; their valiant temper
Men lose when they incline to treachery,
And then they fight like compelled bears, would fly
Were they not tied.

ARCITE.          - Kinsman, you might as well
Speak this and act it in your glass as to
His ear which now disdains you.

PALAMON.                                    Come up to me,
Quit me of these cold gyves, give me a sword,
Though it be rusty, and the charity

Of one meal lend me. Come before me then,
A good sword in thy hand, and do but say
That Emily is thine, I will forgive
The trespass thou hast done me – yea, my life,
If then thou carry't; and brave souls in shades
That have died manly, which will seek of me
Some news from earth, they shall get none but this,
That thou art brave and noble.

ARCITE.                                    Be content;
Again betake you to your hawthorn house.
With counsel of the night, I will be here
With wholesome viands; these impediments
Will I file off; you shall have garments, and
Perfumes to kill the smell o'th'prison. After,
When you shall stretch yourself, and say but 'Arcite,
I am in plight', there shall be at your choice
Both sword and armour.

PALAMON.                    O you heavens, dares any
So noble bear a guilty business? None
But only Arcite; therefore none but Arcite
In this kind is so bold.

ARCITE.                    Sweet Palamon!

PALAMON.
I do embrace you and your offer – for
Your offer do't I only, sir; your person
Without hypocrisy I may not wish
More than my sword's edge on't.

*They wind horns off; cornets sounded.*

ARCITE.                                    You hear the horns;
Enter your muset, lest this match between's
Be crossed ere met. Give me your hand; farewell.
I'll bring you every needful thing; I pray you
Take comfort and be strong.

PALAMON.                                    Pray hold your promise;
And do the deed with a bent brow. Most certain
You love me not; be rough with me, and pour
This oil out of your language; by this air,
I could for each word give a cuff, my stomach
Not reconciled by reason.

ARCITE.                    Plainly spoken.
Yet pardon me hard language; when I spur
My horse, I chide him not; content and anger
In me have but one face.

*They wind horns.*

                                   Hark, sir, they call
The scattered to the banquet; you must guess
I have an office there.

PALAMON.                  Sir, your attendance
Cannot please heaven, and I know your office
Unjustly is achieved.

ARCITE.                I've a good title.
I am persuaded this question, sick between's,
By bleeding must be cured. I am a suitor
That to your sword you will bequeath this plea,
And talk of it no more.

PALAMON.               But this one word.
You are going now to gaze upon my mistress –
For note you, mine she is –

ARCITE.               Nay, then –

PALAMON.                 Nay, pray you.
You talk of feeding me to breed me strength;
You are going now to look upon a sun
That strengthens what it looks on; there you have
A vantage o'er me, but enjoy it till
I may enforce my remedy. Farewell.

*Exeunt.*

## Scene Two

*Enter Gaoler's Daughter alone.*

DAUGHTER.
He has mistook the brake I meant, is gone
After his fancy. 'Tis now wellnigh morning.
No matter; would it were perpetual night,
And darkness lord o'th'world. Hark; 'tis a wolf!
In me hath grief slain fear, and but for one thing
I care for nothing, and that's Palamon.
I reck not if the wolves would jaw me, so
He had this file; what if I hallowed for him?
I cannot hallow; if I whooped, what then?
If he not answered, I should call a wolf,
And do him but that service. I have heard
Strange howls this livelong night; why may't not be
They have made prey of him? He has no weapons;
He cannot run; the jingling of his gyves
Might call fell things to listen, who have in them
A sense to know a man unarmed, and can
Smell where resistance is. I'll set it down

He's torn to pieces; they howled many together,
And then they fed on him; [so much for that.]
Be bold to ring the bell. How stand I then?
All's chared when he is gone. No, no, I lie;
My father's to be hanged for his escape,
Myself to beg, if I prized life so much
As to deny my act; [but that I would not,
Should I try death by dozens.] I am moped;
Food took I none these two days; sipped some water.
I have not closed mine eyes,
Save when my lids scoured off their brine. Alas,
Dissolve, my life; let not my sense unsettle,
Lest I should drown, or stab, or hang myself.
O state of nature, fail together in me,
Since thy best props are warped! So, which way now?
The best way is the next way to a grave;
[Each errant step beside is torment. Lo,]
The moon is down, the crickets chirp, the screech owl
Calls in the dawn. All offices are done,
Save what I fail in; but the point is this,
An end, and that is all.

                                  *Exit.*

## Scene Three

*Enter Arcite, with meat, wine and files*

ARCITE.
I should be near the place. Ho, cousin Palamon!

*Enter Palamon.*

PALAMON.
Arcite?

ARCITE.     The same. I have brought you food and files;
Come forth and fear not, here's no Theseus.

PALAMON.
Nor none so honest, Arcite.

ARCITE.                That's no matter;
We'll argue that hereafter. Come, take courage;
You shall not die thus beastly. Here, sir, drink,
I know you are faint; then I'll talk further with you.

PALAMON.
Arcite, thou mightst now poison me.

ARCITE.                I might;
But I must fear you first. Sit down, and good now,

No more of these vain parleys; let us not,
Having our ancient reputation with us,
Make talk for fools and cowards. To your health!

*He drinks.*

PALAMON.
Do.

ARCITE. Pray sit down then, and let me entreat you,
By all the honesty and honour in you,
No mention of this woman, 'twill disturb us.
We shall have time enough.

PALAMON.                    Well, sir, I'll pledge you.

*He drinks.*

ARCITE.
Drink a good hearty draught, it breeds good blood, man
Do not you feel it thaw you?

PALAMON.                    Stay, I'll tell you
After a draught or two more.

ARCITE.                    Spare it not;
The Duke has more, coz. Eat now.

PALAMON.                    Yes.

*He eats.*

ARCITE.                    I am glad
You have so good a stomach.

PALAMON.                    I am gladder
I have so good meat to't.

ARCITE.                    Is't not mad lodging,
Here in the wild woods, cousin?

PALAMON.                    Yes, for them
That have wild consciences.

ARCITE.                    How tastes your victuals?
Your hunger needs no sauce, I see.

PALAMON.                    Not much;
But if it did, yours is too tart, sweet cousin.
What is this?

ARCITE.          Venison.

PALAMON.                    'Tis a lusty meat;
Give me more wine. Here, Arcite, to the wenches
We have known in our days! The lord steward's daughter –
Do you remember her?

ARCITE.                    After you, coz.

PALAMON.
She loved a black-haired man.

ARCITE.                    She did so; well, sir?

PALAMON.
And I have heard some call him Arcite, and –

ARCITE.
Out with't, faith.

PALAMON.          She met him in an arbour.
What did she there, coz? Play o'th'virginals?

ARCITE.
Something she did, sir.

PALAMON.                    Made her groan a month for't –
Or two, or three, or ten.

ARCITE.                    The marshal's sister
Had her share too, as I remember, cousin,
Else there be tales abroad; you'll pledge her?

PALAMON.                    Yes.

ARCITE.
A pretty brown wench 'tis. There was a time
When young men went a-hunting – and a wood,
And a broad beech – and thereby hangs a tale –
Heigh ho!

PALAMON.     For Emily, upon my life! Fool,
Away with this strained mirth; I say again,
That sigh was breathed for Emily. Base cousin,
Darest thou break first?

ARCITE.          You are wide.

PALAMON.                    By heaven and earth,
There's nothing in thee honest.

ARCITE.                    Then I'll leave you;
You are a beast now.

PALAMON.                    As thou makest me, traitor.

ARCITE.
There's all things needful; files, and shirts, and perfumes.
I'll come again some two hours hence, and bring
That that shall quiet all.

PALAMON.                    A sword and armour!

ARCITE.
Fear me not. You are now too foul; farewell.

Get off your trinkets; you shall want naught.

PALAMON.                                        Sirrah –

ARCITE.
     I'll hear no more.

                                                        *Exit.*

PALAMON.          If he keep touch, he dies for't.

                                                        *Exit.*


## Scene Four

*Enter Gaoler's Daughter.*

DAUGHTER.
     I am very cold, and all the stars are out too,
     The little stars and all, that look like aglets.
     The sun has seen my folly. Palamon!
     Alas, no; he's in heaven. Where am I now?
     Yonder's the sea, and there's a ship; how't tumbles!
     And there's a rock lies watching under water;
     [Now, now, it beats upon it; now, now, now,]
     There's a leak sprung, a sound one; how they cry!
     Spoon her before the wind, you'll lose all else;
     Up with a course or two, and tack about, boys.
     Good night, good night, you're gone. I am very hungry.
     Would I could find a fine frog; he would tell me
     News from all parts o'th'world; then would I make
     A carrack of a cockleshell, and sail
     By east and north-east to the King of Pygmies,
     For he tells fortunes rarely. Now my father,
     Twenty to one, is trussed up in a trice
     Tomorrow morning; I'll say never a word.

     *She sings.*

     For I'll cut my green coat, a foot above my knee,
     And I'll clip my yellow locks an inch below mine ee;
                              Hey, nonny, nonny, nonny.
     He s' buy me a white cut, forth for to ride,
     And I'll go seek him, through the world that is so wide;
                              Hey, nonny, nonny, nonny.

     O for a prick now, like a nightingale,
     To put my breast against; I shall sleep like a top else.

                                                        *Exit.*


## Scene Five

*Enter a Schoolmaster, six Countrymen, one dressed as a bavian, and five wenches, with a Taborer.*

SCHOOLMASTER.
     Fie, fie,
     What tediosity and disinsanity
     Is here among ye! Have my rudiments
     Been laboured so long with ye, milked unto ye,
     And, by a figure, even the very plum-broth
     And marrow of my understanding laid upon ye?
     And do you still cry 'Where?' and 'How?' and 'Wherefore?'
     [You most coarse frieze capacities, ye jean judgements,
     Have I said 'Thus let be', and 'There let be',
     And 'Then let be', and no man understand me?]
     *Proh deum, medius fidius*, ye are all dunces!
     Forwhy, here stand I; here the Duke comes; there are you
     Close in the thicket. The Duke appears; I meet him,
     And unto him I utter learnèd things,
     And many figures; he hears and nods, and hums,
     And then cries 'Rare!', and I go forward; at length
     I fling my cap up – mark there! – then do you,
     As once did Meleager and the boar,
     Break comely out before him; like true lovers,
     Cast yourselves in a body decently,
     And sweetly, by a figure, trace and turn, boys.

FIRST COUNTRYMAN.
     And sweetly we will do it, Master Gerrold.

[1] [SECOND ]COUNTRYMAN.
     Draw up the company. Where's the [2][taborer?

THIRD COUNTRYMAN.
     Why, Timothy!

TABORER.          Here, my mad boys; have at ye!

SCHOOLMASTER.
     But, I say, where's their women?

FOURTH COUNTRYMAN.          Here's Friz and Maudline.]

[3] [SECOND COUNTRYMAN.
     And] little Luce with the white legs, and bouncing Barbary.

[4] [FIRST ]COUNTRYMAN.
     And freckled Nell, that never failed her master.

SCHOOLMASTER.
     Where be your ribands, maids? Swim with your bodies,
     And carry it sweetly and deliverly,
     And now and then a favour and a frisk.

NELL.
        Let us alone, sir.

[SCHOOLMASTER.        Where's the rest o'th'music?

THIRD COUNTRYMAN.
        Dispersed as you commanded.]

SCHOOLMASTER.                Couple then,
        And see what's wanting. Where's the bavian?
        My friend, carry your tail without offence
        Or scandal to the ladies; and be sure
        You tumble with audacity and manhood,
        And when you bark do it with judgement.

BAVIAN.                        Yes, sir.

SCHOOLMASTER.
        *Quousque tandem?* Here is a woman wanting!

*[FOURTH COUNTRYMAN.
        We may go whistle; all the fat's i'th'fire.]

SCHOOLMASTER.
        We have,
        As learnèd authors utter, washed a tile;
        We have been *fatuus*, and laboured vainly.

*[SECOND] COUNTRYMAN.
        This is that scornful piece, that scurvy hilding,
        That gave her promise faithfully she would
        Be here – Cicely, the sempster's daughter;
        The next gloves that I give her shall be dogskin!
        [Nay, an she fail me once – you can tell, Arcas,]
        She swore by wine and bread she would not break.

SCHOOLMASTER.
        An eel and woman,
        A learnèd poet says, unless by th'tail
        And with thy teeth thou hold, will either fail.
        [In manners this was false position.

FIRST COUNTRYMAN.
        A fire-ill take her; does she flinch now?]

THIRD COUNTRYMAN.                What
        Shall we determine, sir?

SCHOOLMASTER.        Nothing;
        Our business is become a nullity,
        Yea, and a woeful and a piteous nullity.

FOURTH COUNTRYMAN.
        Now, when the credit of our town lay on it,
        [Now to be frampold, now to piss o'th'nettle!

Go thy ways, I'll remember thee; I'll fit thee.]

*Enter Gaoler's Daughter.*

DAUGHTER (*sings*).
                The *George Alow* came from the south,
                        From the coast of Barbary-a;
                And there he met with brave gallants of war,
                        By one, by two, by three-a

                Well hailed, well hailed, you jolly gallants,
                        And whither now are you bound-a?
                O, let me have your company
                        Till I come to the sound-a.
        There was three fools fell out about an owlet;

*She sings.*

                The one he said it was an owl,
                        The other he said nay;
                The third he said it was a hawk,
                        And her bells were cut away.

[7][THIRD ] COUNTRYMAN.
        There's a dainty madwoman, master,
        Comes i'th'nick, as mad as a March hare.
        If we can get her dance, we are made again;
        I warrant her, she'll do the rarest gambols.

FIRST COUNTRYMAN.
        A madwoman? We are made, boys!

SCHOOLMASTER.
        And are you mad, good woman?

DAUGHTER.                I would be sorry else.
        Give me your hand.

SCHOOLMASTER.        Why?

DAUGHTER.                I can tell your fortune.
        You are a fool. Tell ten; I have posed him. Buzz!
        Friend, you must eat no white bread; if you do,
        Your teeth will bleed extremely. Shall we dance, ho?
        I know you, you're a tinker; sirrah tinker,
        Stop no more holes but what you should.

SCHOOLMASTER.                *Dii boni*,
        A tinker, damsel?

DAUGHTER.                Or a conjurer;
        Raise me a devil now, and let him play
        *Chi passa* o'th'bells and bones.

SCHOOLMASTER.                Go take her,
        And fluently persuade her to a peace.

[*Et opus exegi, quod nec Iovis ira nec ignis –*]
Strike up, and lead her in.

[SECOND] COUNTRYMAN. [8]                   Come, lass, let's trip it.

DAUGHTER.
I'll lead.

THIRD COUNTRYMAN. Do, do.

SCHOOLMASTER.
Persuasively and cunningly! Away, boys.

*Horns sound within.*

I hear the horns; give me some meditation,
And mark your cue.

                    *Exeunt all but Schoolmaster.*

             Pallas inspire me!

*Enter Theseus, Pirithous, Hippolyta, Emilia, Arcite, and train.*

THESEUS.
This way the stag took.

SCHOOLMASTER.            Stay, and edify!

THESEUS.
What have we here?

PIRITHOUS.           Some country sport, upon my life, sir.

THESEUS.
Well, sir, go forward, we will edify.
Ladies, sit down; we'll stay it.

*A chair and stools are brought out; the ladies sit.*

SCHOOLMASTER.
Thou doughty Duke, all hail; all hail, sweet ladies!

THESEUS.
This is a cold beginning.

SCHOOLMASTER.
If you but favour, our country pastime made is.
We are a few of those collected here
That ruder tongues distinguish villager;
And to say verity, and not to fable,
We are a merry rout, or else a rabble,
Or company, or, by a figure, *chorus,*
That 'fore thy dignity will dance a morris.
And I that am the rectifier of all,
By title *pedagogus,* that let fall
The birch upon the breeches of the small ones,
And humble with a ferula the tall ones,

Do here present this machine, or this frame;
And, dainty Duke, whose doughty dismal fame
From Dis to Daedalus, from post to pillar,
Is blown abroad, help me, thy poor well-willer,
And with thy twinkling eyes look right and straight
Upon this mighty 'Morr', of mickle weight;
'Is' now comes in, which being glued together
Makes 'Morris', and the cause that we came hither,
The body of our sport, of no small study.
I first appear, though rude, and raw, and muddy,
To speak before thy noble grace this tenor,
At whose great feet I offer up my penner;
The next, the Lord of May and Lady bright;
The chambermaid and servingman, by night
That seek out silent hanging; then mine host
And his fat spouse, that welcomes to their cost
The gallèd traveller, and with a beckoning
Informs the tapster to inflame the reckoning;
Then the beest-eating clown, and next the fool,
The bavian, with long tail and eke long tool,
*Cum multis aliis* that make a dance;
Say 'ay', and all shall presently advance.

THESEUS.
Ay, ay, by any means, dear dominie.

PIRITHOUS.
Produce!

SCHOOLMASTER.
*Intrate, filii!* Come forth and foot it.

*Schoolmaster knocks; enter the dancers. Music is played; they dance.*

Ladies, if we have been merry,
And have pleased ye with a derry,
And a derry, and a down,
Say the schoolmaster's no clown;
Duke, if we have pleased thee too,
And have done as good boys should do,
Give us but a tree or twain
For a maypole, and again,
Ere another year run out,
We'll make thee laugh, and all this rout.

THESEUS.
Take twenty, dominie. (*To Hippolyta:*) How does my
    sweetheart?

HIPPOLYTA.
Never so pleased, sir.

EMILIA.                              'Twas an excellent dance,
    And for a preface I never heard a better.

THESEUS.
    Schoolmaster, I thank you. – One see 'em all rewarded.

PIRITHOUS.
    And here's something to paint your pole withal.

THESEUS.
    Now to our sports again.

SCHOOLMASTER.
    May the stag thou huntest stand long,
    And thy dogs be swift and strong;
    May they kill him without lets,
    And the ladies eat his dowsets.

    *Horns sound. Exeunt Theseus, Pirithous, Hippolyta, Emilia,*
    *Arcite, and train.*

    Come, we are all made. *Dii deaeque omnes,*
    Ye have danced rarely, wenches.

                                                    *Exeunt.*


## Scene Six

*Enter Palamon from the bush.*

PALAMON.
    About this hour my cousin gave his faith
    To visit me again, and with him bring
    Two swords and two good armours; if he fail,
    He's neither man nor soldier. When he left me,
    I did not think a week could have restored
    My lost strength to me, I was grown so low
    And crestfallen with my wants. I thank thee, Arcite,
    Thou art yet a fair foe; and I feel myself,
    With this refreshing, able once again
    To outdure danger. To delay it longer
    Would make the world think, when it comes to hearing,
    That I lay fatting like a swine to fight,
    And not a soldier. Therefore this blest morning
    Shall be the last; [and that sword he refuses,
    If it but hold, I kill him with; 'tis justice.]
    So, love and fortune for me!

    *Enter Arcite with armours and swords.*

                            O, good morrow.

ARCITE.
    Good morrow, noble kinsman.

PALAMON.                              I have put you
    To too much pains, sir.

ARCITE.                          That too much, fair cousin,
    Is but a debt to honour, and my duty.

PALAMON.
    Would you were so in all, sir; I could wish ye
    As kind a kinsman as you force me find
    A beneficial foe, that my embraces
    Might thank ye, not my blows.

ARCITE.                              [I shall think either,
    Well done, a noble recompense.

PALAMON.                              Then I shall quit you.

ARCITE.
    Defy me in these fair terms, and you show
    More than a mistress to me; no more anger,
    As you love anything that's honourable!]
    We were not bred to talk, man; when we are armed,
    And both upon our guards, then let our fury,
    Like meeting of two tides, fly strongly from us,
    And then to whom the birthright of this beauty
    Truly pertains – without upbraidings, scorns,
    Despisings of our persons, and such poutings
    Fitter for girls and schoolboys – will be seen,
    And quickly, yours or mine. Will't please you arm, sir?
    Or if you feel yourself not fitting yet
    And furnished with your old strength, I'll stay, cousin,
    And every day discourse you into health,
    As I am spared. Your person I am friends with,
    And I could wish I had not said I loved her,
    Though I had died; but loving such a lady,
    And justifying my love, I must not fly from't.

PALAMON.
    Arcite, thou art so brave an enemy
    That no man but thy cousin's fit to kill thee.
    I am well and lusty. Choose your arms.

ARCITE.                              Choose you, sir.

PALAMON.
    Wilt thou exceed in all, or dost thou do't
    To make me spare thee?

ARCITE.                          If you think so, cousin,
    You are deceived, for as I am a soldier
    I will not spare you.

PALAMON.                    That's well said.

ARCITE.                              You'll find it.

PALAMON.
Then as I am an honest man and love,
With all the justice of affection
I'll pay thee soundly. This I'll take.

*He chooses his armour.*

ARCITE.                              That's mine then.
I'll arm you first.

PALAMON.              Do. Pray thee tell me, cousin,
Where gottest thou this good armour?

ARCITE.                              'Tis the Duke's,
And to say true, I stole it. Do I pinch you?

PALAMON.
No.

ARCITE.  Is't not too heavy?

PALAMON.              I have worn a lighter,
But I shall make it serve.

ARCITE.              I'll buckle't close.

PALAMON.
By any means.

ARCITE.              You care not for a grand guard?

PALAMON.
No, no, we'll use no horses. I perceive
You would fain be at that fight.

ARCITE.                    I am indifferent.

PALAMON.
Faith, so am I. Good cousin, thrust the buckle
Through far enough.

ARCITE.              I warrant you.

PALAMON.                        My casque now.

ARCITE.
Will you fight bare-armed?

PALAMON.              We shall be the nimbler.

ARCITE.
But use your gauntlets, though. Those are o'th'least;
Prithee take mine, good cousin.

PALAMON.              Thank you, Arcite.

How do I look? Am I fallen much away?

ARCITE.
Faith, very little; love has used you kindly.

PALAMON.
I'll warrant thee I'll strike home,

ARCITE.                        Do, and spare not;
I'll give you cause, sweet cousin.

PALAMON.                    Now to you, sir.

*He arms Arcite.*

Methinks this armour's very like that, Arcite,
Thou worest that day the three kings fell, but lighter.

ARCITE.
That was a very good one, and that day,
I well remember, you outdid me, cousin.
I never saw such valour; when you charged
Upon the left wing of the enemy,
I spurred hard to come up, and under me
I had a right good horse.

PALAMON.              You had indeed;
A bright bay, I remember.

ARCITE.                    Yes, but all
Was vainly laboured in me; you outwent me,
Nor could my wishes reach you; yet a little
I did by imitation.

PALAMON.              More by virtue;
You are modest, cousin.

[ARCITE.                    When I saw you charge first,
Methought I heard a dreadful clap of thunder
Break from the troop.]

PALAMON.                    [But still before that flew
The lightning of your valour.] Stay a little;
Is not this piece too strait?

ARCITE.                    No, no, 'tis well.

PALAMON.
I would have nothing hurt thee but my sword;
A bruise would be dishonour.

ARCITE.                    Now I am perfect.

PALAMON.
Stand off then.

ARCITE.              Take my sword; I hold it better.

PALAMON.

I thank ye. No, keep it, your life lies on it.
Here's one; if it but hold, I ask no more,
For all my hopes. My cause and honour guard me!

ARCITE.

And me my love!

*They bow several ways, then advance and stand.*

Is there aught else to say?

PALAMON.

This only, [1][and no more. Thou art mine aunt's son,
And that blood] we desire to shed is mutual,
In me, thine, and in thee, mine; my sword
Is in my hand, and if thou killest me
The gods and I forgive thee. If there be
A place prepared for those that sleep in honour,
I wish his weary soul that falls may win it.
Fight bravely, cousin; give me thy noble hand.

ARCITE.

Here, Palamon. This hand shall never more
Come near thee with such friendship.

PALAMON.                                    I commend thee.

ARCITE.

[If I fall, curse me, and say I was a coward,
For none but such dare die in these just trials.]
One more farewell, my cousin.

PALAMON.                                    Farewell, Arcite.

*They fight. Then horns sound within; they stand.*

ARCITE.

Lo, cousin, lo, our folly has undone us!

PALAMON.

Why?

ARCITE.    This is the Duke, a-hunting [as I told you;
If we be found, we are wretchèd.] O, retire
For honour's sake, and safety, presently
Into your bush again, sir; we shall find
Too many hours to die in. Gentle cousin,
If you be seen you perish instantly
For breaking prison, and I, if you reveal me,
For my contempt; then all the world will scorn us,
And say we had a noble difference,
But base disposers of it.

PALAMON.                         No, no, cousin,

I will no more be hidden, nor put off
This great adventure to a second trial.
I know your cunning, [and I know your cause;
He that faints now, shame take him! Put thyself
Upon thy present guard.]

ARCITE.                              [2]You are not mad?

PALAMON.

[Or I will make th'advantage of this hour
Mine own, and what to come shall threaten me
I fear less than my fortune.] Know, weak cousin,
I love Emilia, and in that I'll bury
Thee, and all crosses else.

ARCITE.                              [Then come what can come,
Thou shalt know, Palamon, I dare as well
Die as discourse or sleep; only this fears me,
The law will have the honour of our ends.]
Have at thy life!

PALAMON.              Look to thine own well, Arcite.

*They fight again. Horns sound within; enter Theseus, Hippolyta,
Emilia, Pirithous, and train.*

THESEUS.

What ignorant and mad malicious traitors
Are you, that 'gainst the tenor of my laws
Are making battle, thus like knights appointed,
Without my leave and officers of arms?
By Castor, both shall die.

PALAMON.                              Hold thy word, Theseus;
We are certainly both traitors, both despisers
Of thee, and of thy goodness. I am Palamon
That cannot love thee, he that broke thy prison –
Think well what that deserves – and this is Arcite;
A bolder traitor never trod thy ground,
A falser ne'er seemed friend; this is the man
Was begged and banished, this is he contemns thee
And what thou darest do, and in this disguise,
Against thine own edict follows thy sister,
That fortunate bright star, the fair Emilia –
Whose servant, if there be a right in seeing,
And first bequeathing of the soul to, justly
I am – and which is more, dares think her his.
This treachery, like a most trusty lover,
I called him now to answer; if thou be'st
As thou art spoken, great and virtuous,
The true decider of all injuries,
Say 'Fight again', and thou shalt see me, Theseus,

Do such a justice thou thyself wilt envy.
Then take my life; I'll woo thee to't.

PIRITHOUS.                              O heaven,
What more than man is this!

THESEUS.                         I have sworn.

ARCITE.                                   We seek not
Thy breath of mercy, Theseus; ['tis to me
A thing as soon to die as thee to say it,
And no more moved.] Where this man calls me traitor,
Let me say thus much: if in love be treason,
In service of so excellent a beauty,
As I love most, and in that faith will perish,
As I have brought my life here to confirm it,
As I have served her truest, worthiest,
As I dare kill this cousin that denies it,
So let me be most traitor, and ye please me.
For scorning thy edict, Duke, ask that lady
Why she is fair, and why her eyes command me.
Stay here to love her; and if she say 'traitor',
I am a villain fit to lie unburied.

PALAMON.
Thou shalt have pity of us both, O Theseus,
3[If unto neither thou show mercy. Stop,
As thou art just, thy noble ear against us;
As thou art valiant, for thy cousin's soul,
Whose twelve strong labours crown his memory,]
Let's die together, at one instant, Duke;
Only a little let him fall before me,
That I may tell my soul he shall not have her.

THESEUS.
I grant your wish, for to say true your cousin
Has ten times more offended, for I gave him
More mercy than you found, sir, your offences
Being no more than his. None here speak for 'em;
For ere the sun set, both shall sleep for ever.

HIPPOLYTA.
Alas, the pity! Now or never, sister,
Speak not to be denied; that face of yours
Will bear the curses else of after ages
For these lost cousins.

EMILIA.                         In my face, dear sister,
I find no anger to 'em, nor no ruin;
The misadventure of their own eyes kill 'em.
Yet that I will be woman and have pity,
My knees shall grow to th'ground but I'll get mercy.

Help me, dear sister; in a deed so virtuous,
The powers of all women will be with us.

*The ladies kneel.*

Most royal brother –

HIPPOLYTA.                    Sir, by our tie of marriage –

EMILIA.
By your own spotless honour –

HIPPOLYTA.                         By that faith,
That fair hand, and that honest heart you gave me –

EMILIA.
By that you would have pity in another,
By your own virtues infinite –

HIPPOLYTA.                         By valour,
By all the chaste nights I have ever pleased you –

THESEUS.
These are strange conjurings.

PIRITHOUS.                         Nay, then I'll in too;
By all our friendship, sir, by all our dangers,
By all you love most, wars and this sweet lady –

EMILIA.
By that you would have trembled to deny
A blushing maid –

HIPPOLYTA.                    By your own eyes; by strength
In which you swore I went beyond all women,
Almost all men, and yet I yielded, Theseus –

PIRITHOUS.
To crown all this; by your most noble soul,
Which cannot want due mercy, I beg first –

HIPPOLYTA.
Next hear my prayers –

EMILIA.                         Last let me entreat, sir –

PIRITHOUS.
For mercy.

HIPPOLYTA.          Mercy.

EMILIA.                    Mercy on these princes!

THESEUS.
Ye make my faith reel. Say I felt
Compassion to 'em both, how would you place it?

EMILIA.
Upon their lives – but with their banishments.

THESEUS.
You are a right woman, sister; you have pity,
But want the understanding where to use it.
If you desire their lives, invent a way
Safer than banishment; can these two live,
And have the agony of love about 'em,
And not kill one another? Every day
They'd fight about you, hourly bring your honour
In public question with their swords. Be wise then,
And here forget 'em; it concerns your credit
And my oath equally; I have said they die.
Better they fall by th'law than one another.
Bow not my honour.

EMILIA.                    O, my noble brother,
That oath was rashly made, and in your anger;
[Your reason will not hold it. If such vows
Stand for express will, all the world must perish.]
Beside, I have another oath 'gainst yours,
Of more authority, I am sure more love;
Not made in passion neither, but good heed.

THESEUS.
What is it, sister?

PIRITHOUS.          Urge it home, brave lady.

EMILIA.
That you would ne'er deny me anything
Fit for my modest suit, and your free granting.
[I tie you to your word now; if ye fall in't,
Think how you maim your honour –
For now I am set a-begging, sir, I am deaf
To all but your compassion – how their lives
Might breed the ruin of my name, opinion.]
Shall anything that loves me perish for me?
That were a cruel wisdom; do men prune
The straight young boughs that blush with thousand blossoms
Because they may be rotten? O Duke Theseus,
The goodly mothers that have groaned for these,
And all the longing maids that ever loved 'em,
If your vow stand, shall curse me and my beauty,
And in their funeral songs for these two cousins
Despise my cruelty, and cry woe worth me,
Till I am nothing but the scorn of women;
For heaven's sake, save their lives and banish 'em.

THESEUS.
On what conditions?

EMILIA.                    Swear 'em never more
To make me their contention, or to know me,
To tread upon thy dukedom, and to be,
Wherever they shall travel, ever strangers
To one another.

PALAMON.          I'll be cut a-pieces
Before I take this oath! Forget I love her?
O all ye gods, despise me then. Thy banishment
I not mislike, so we may fairly carry
Our swords and cause along; else never trifle,
But take our lives, Duke. I must love and will,
And for that love must and dare kill this cousin
On any piece the earth has.

THESEUS.                    Will you, Arcite,
Take these conditions?

PALAMON.                    He's a villain, then.

PIRITHOUS.
These are men!

ARCITE.
No, never, Duke; 'tis worse to me than begging
To take my life so basely. Though I think
I shall never enjoy her, yet I'll preserve
The honour of affection and die for her,
Make death a devil.

THESEUS.
What may be done? For now I feel compassion.

*The ladies rise.*

PIRITHOUS.
Let it not fall again, sir.

THESEUS.                    Say, Emilia,
If one of them were dead, as one must, are you
Content to take the other to your husband?
They cannot both enjoy you. They are princes
As goodly as your own eyes, and as noble
As ever fame yet spoke of; look upon 'em,
And if you can love, end this difference.
I give consent; are you content too, princes?

PALAMON *and* ARCITE.
With all our souls.

THESEUS.                    He that she refuses
Must die then.

PALAMON *and* ARCITE.
                    Any death thou canst invent, Duke.

[PALAMON.
If I fall from that mouth, I fall with favour,
And lovers yet unborn shall bless my ashes.

ARCITE.
If she refuse me, yet my grave will wed me,
And soldiers sing my epitaph.]

THESEUS.                                 Make choice then.

EMILIA.
I cannot, sir, they are both too excellent;
For me, a hair shall never fall of these men.

HIPPOLYTA.
What will become of 'em?

THESEUS.                          Thus I ordain it,
And by mine honour once again, it stands,
Or both shall die: you shall both to your country,
And each within this month, accompanied
With three fair knights, appear again in this place,
In which I'll plant a pyramid; and whether,
Before us that are here, can force his cousin
By fair and knightly strength to touch the pillar,
He shall enjoy her; the other lose his head,
And all his friends; nor shall he grudge to fall,
Nor think he dies with interest in this lady.
Will this content ye?

PALAMON.                     Yes! – Here, cousin Arcite,
I am friends again, till that hour.

ARCITE.                                 I embrace ye.

THESEUS.
Are you content, sister?

EMILIA.                          Yes, I must, sir,
Else both miscarry.

THESEUS.                     Come, shake hands again then,
And take heed, as you are gentlemen, this quarrel
Sleep till the hour prefixed, and hold your course.

PALAMON.
We dare not fail thee, Theseus.

THESEUS.                              Come, I'll give ye
Now usage like to princes and to friends.
When ye return, who wins, I'll settle here;
Who loses, yet I'll weep upon his bier.

*Exeunt*

# ACT FOUR

## Scene One

*Enter Gaoler and his Friend.*

GAOLER.
Heard you no more? Was nothing said of me
Concerning the escape of Palamon?
Good sir, remember.

FIRST FRIEND.                Nothing that I heard,
For I came home before the business
Was fully ended. Yet I might perceive,
Ere I departed, a great likelihood
Of both their pardons; for Hippolyta
And fair-eyed Emily, upon their knees,
Begged with such handsome pity that the Duke
Methought stood staggering, whether he should follow
His rash oath or the sweet compassion
Of those two ladies; and to second them
That truly noble prince Pirithous,
Half his own heart, set in too, that I hope
All shall be well; neither heard I one question
Of your name, or his 'scape.

GAOLER.                              Pray heaven it hold so!

*Enter Second Friend.*

SECOND FRIEND.
Be of good comfort, man; I bring you news,
Good news.

GAOLER.        They are welcome.

SECOND FRIEND.                     Palamon has cleared you,
And got your pardon, and discovered how
And by whose means he escaped, which was your daughter's,
Whose pardon is procured too; and the prisoner,
Not to be held ungrateful to her goodness,
Has given a sum of money to her marriage,
A large one, I'll assure you.

GAOLER.                          Ye are a good man
And ever bring good news.

FIRST FRIEND.                     How was it ended?

SECOND FRIEND.
Why, as it should be; they that never begged
But they prevailed had their suits fairly granted;

The prisoners have their lives.

FIRST FRIEND.                    I knew 'twould be so.

SECOND FRIEND.
But there be new conditions, which you'll hear of
At better time.

GAOLER.          I hope they are good.

SECOND FRIEND.                    They are honourable;
How good they'll prove I know not.

FIRST FRIEND.                    'Twill be known.

*Enter Wooer.*

WOOER.
Alas, sir, where's your daughter?

GAOLER.                    Why do you ask?

WOOER.
O sir, when did you see her?

SECOND FRIEND.                    How he looks!

GAOLER.
This morning.

WOOER.          Was she well? Was she in health, sir?
When did she sleep?

FIRST FRIEND.          These are strange questions.

GOALER.
I do not think she was very well, for now
You make me mind her, but this very day
I asked her questions, and she answered me
So far from what she was, so childishly,
So sillily, as if she were a fool,
An innocent, and I was very angry.
But what of her, sir?

WOOER.          Nothing but my pity;
But you must know it, and as good by me
As by another that less loves her –

GAOLER.
Well, sir?

FIRST FRIEND.  Not right?

SECOND FRIEND.          Not well?

WOOER.          No, sir, not well.
'Tis too true, she is mad.

FIRST FRIEND.          It cannot be

WOOER.
Believe you'll find it so.

GAOLER.                    I half suspected
What you have told me; the gods comfort her!
Either this was her love to Palamon,
Or fear of my miscarrying on his 'scape,
Or both.

WOOER.          'Tis likely.

GAOLER.                    But why all this haste, sir?

WOOER.
I'll tell you quickly. As I late was angling
In the great lake that lies behind the palace,
From the far shore, thick-set with reeds and sedges,
[As patiently I was attending sport,]
I heard a voice, a shrill one; and attentive
I gave my ear, when I might well perceive
'Twas one that sung, and by the smallness of it
A boy or woman. I then left my angle
To his own skill, came near, but yet perceived not
Who made the sound, the rushes and the reeds
Had so encompassed it. I laid me down
And listened to the words she sung, for then,
Through a small glade cut by the fishermen,
I saw it was your daughter.

GAOLER.                    Pray go on, sir.

WOOER.
She sung much, but no sense; only I heard her
Repeat this often: 'Palamon is gone,
Is gone to th'wood to gather mulberries;
I'll find him out tomorrow.'

FIRST FRIEND.                    Pretty soul!

WOOER.
'His shackles will betray him; he'll be taken,
And what shall I do then? I'll bring a bevy,
A hundred black-eyed maids, that love as I do,
[With chaplets on their heads of daffadillies,]
With cherry lips and cheeks of damask roses,
And all we'll dance an antic 'fore the Duke,
And beg his pardon.' Then she talked of you, sir;
That you must lose your heard tomorrow morning,
And she must gather flowers to bury you,
And see the house made handsome. Then she sung
Nothing but 'Willow, willow, willow', and between
Ever was 'Palamon, fair Palamon',
[And 'Palamon was a tall young man.'] The place

Was knee-deep where she sat; her careless tresses
A wreath of bulrush rounded; about her stuck
Thousand fresh water flowers of several colours,
That methought she appeared like the fair nymph
That feeds the lake with waters, [or as Iris
Newly dropped down from heaven.] Rings she made
Of rushes that grew by, and to 'em spoke
The prettiest posies, 'Thus our true love's tied',
'This you may lose, not me', and many a one.
And then she wept, and sung again, and sighed,
And with the same breath smiled and kissed her hand.

SECOND FRIEND.
Alas, what pity it is!

WOOER.                    I made in to her;
She saw me, and straight sought the flood. I saved her,
And set her safe to land; when presently
She slipped away, and to the city made
With such a cry and swiftness that, believe me,
She left me far behind her. Three or four
I saw from far off cross her – one of 'em
I knew to be your brother – where she stayed,
And fell, scarce to be got away. I left them with her,
And hither came to tell you.

*Enter Gaoler's Brother, Gaoler's Daughter, and others.*

                    Here they are.

DAUGHTER (*sings*).
        May you never more enjoy the light, *etc.*
Is not this a fine song?

BROTHER.                O, a very fine one.

DAUGHTER.
I can sing twenty more.

BROTHER.                I think you can.

DAUGHTER.
Yes, truly can I; I can sing 'The Broom',
And 'Bonny Robin'. Are you not a tailor?

BROTHER.
Yes.

DAUGHTER. Where's my wedding gown?

BROTHER.                    I'll bring it tomorrow.

DAUGHTER.
Do, very early; I must be abroad else
To call the maids, and pay the minstrels.

For I must lose my maidenhead by cocklight;
'Twill never thrive else.

*She sings.*

            O fair, O sweet, *etc.*

BROTHER.
You must e'en take it patiently.

GAOLER.                            'Tis true.

DAUGHTER.
Good e'en, good men. Pray did you ever hear
Of one young Palamon?

GAOLER.                    Yes, wench, we know him.

DAUGHTER.
Is't not a fine young gentleman?

GAOLER.                        'Tis, love.

BROTHER.
By no mean cross her; she is then distempered
Far worse than now she shows.

[1][FIRST FRIEND.]                    Yes, he's a fine man.

DAUGHTER.
O, is he so? You have a sister.

[1][FIRST FRIEND.]                        Yes.

DAUGHTER.
But she shall never have him, tell her so,
For a trick that I know. You'd best look to her;
For if she see him once, she's gone, she's done,
And undone in an hour. All the young maids
Of our town are in love with him, but I laugh at 'em,
And let 'em all alone; is't not a wise course?

FIRST FRIEND.                        Yes.

DAUGHTER.
There is at least two hundred now with child by him –
There must be four; yet I keep close for all this,
Close as a cockle; and all these must be boys –
He has the trick on't – and at ten years old
They must be all gelt for musicians,
And sing the wars of Theseus.

SECOND FRIEND.                    This is strange.

DAUGHTER.
As ever you heard; but say nothing.

FIRST FRIEND.                        No.

DAUGHTER.
    They come from all parts of the dukedom to him.
    I'll warrant ye, he had not so few last night
    As twenty to dispatch; he'll tickle it up
    In two hours, if his hand be in.

GAOLER.                       She's lost
    Past all cure.

BROTHER.        Heaven forbid, man!

DAUGHTER (to Gaoler).
    Come hither; you are a wise man.

FIRST FRIEND.             Does she know him?

SECOND FRIEND.
    No, would she did.

DAUGHTER.       You are master of a ship?

GAOLER.
    Yes.

DAUGHTER. Where's your compass?

GAOLER.                Here.

DAUGHTER.            Set it to th'north;
    And now direct your course to th'wood, where Palamon
    Lies longing for me. For the tackling
    Let me alone. Come, weigh, my hearts, cheerily!

ALL THE OTHERS.
    O, O, O!

DAUGHTER.
    'Tis up. The wind's fair; top the bowling;
    Out with the mainsail! Where's your whistle, master?

BROTHER.
    Let's get her in.

GAOLER.        Up to the top, boy.

BROTHER.            Where's
    The pilot?

FIRST FRIEND.  Here.

DAUGHTER.     What kennest thou?

SECOND FRIEND.         A fair wood.

DAUGHTER.
    Bear for it, master; tack about!

*She sings.*

When Cynthia with her borrowed light, *etc.*

                              *Exeunt.*

## Scene Two

*Enter Emilia alone, with two pictures.*

EMILIA.
    Yet I may bind those wounds up, that must open
    And bleed to death for my sake else; I'll choose,
    And end their strife. Two such young handsome men
    Shall never fall for me; their weeping mothers,
    Following the dead cold ashes of their sons,
    Shall never curse my cruelty. Good heaven,
    What a sweet face has Arcite! If wise Nature
    With all her best endowments, all those beauties
    She sows into the births of noble bodies,
    Were here a mortal woman, and had in her
    The coy denials of young maids, yet doubtless
    She would run mad for this man. What an eye,
    Of what a fiery sparkle and quick sweetness,
    Has this young prince! Here love himself sits smiling.
    [1][Just such another, wanton Ganymede
    Set Jove afire with, and enforced the god
    Snatch up the goodly boy, and set him by him,
    A shining constellation. What a brow,
    Of what a spacious majesty, he carries,
    Arched like the great-eyed Juno's, but far sweeter,
    Smoother than Pelops' shoulder! Fame and honour,
    Methinks, from hence, as from a promontory
    Pointed in heaven, should clap their wings, and sing
    To all the under world the loves and fights
    Of gods and such men near 'em. Palamon
    Is but his foil; to him, a mere dull shadow.]
    He's swarth and meagre, of an eye as heavy
    As if he had lost his mother; a still temper,
    No stirring in him, no alacrity,
    Of all this sprightly sharpness not a smile.
    Yet these that we count errors may become him;
    Narcissus was a sad boy, but a heavenly.
    O, who can find the bent of woman's fancy?
    I am a fool; my reason is lost in me,
    I have no choice, and I have lied so lewdly
    That women ought to beat me. On my knees
    I ask thy pardon; Palamon, thou art alone
    And only beautiful, and these the eyes,
    These the bright lamps of beauty, that command

And threaten love, and what young maid dare cross 'em?
[What a bold gravity, and yet inviting,
Has this brown manly face! O love, this only
From this hour is complexion.] Lie there, Arcite;
Thou art a changeling to him, a mere gypsy,
And this the noble body. I am sotted,
Utterly lost; my virgin's faith has fled me.
For if my brother but even now had asked me
Whether I loved, I had run mad for Arcite;
Now if my sister, more for Palamon.
Stand both together. Now come ask me, brother –
Alas, I know not! Ask me now, sweet sister;
I may go look. What a mere child is fancy,
That having two fair gauds of equal sweetness,
Cannot distinguish, but must cry for both!

*Enter* [2][*a Gentleman.*]

How now, sir?

[2][GENTLEMAN.]          From the noble Duke your brother,
Madam, I bring you news; the knights are come.

EMILIA.
    To end the quarrel?

[2][GENTLEMAN.]                Yes.

EMILIA.                            Would I might end first!
What sins have I committed, chaste Diana,
That my unspotted youth must now be soiled
With blood of princes, and my chastity
Be made the altar where the lives of lovers –
[Two greater and two better never yet
Made mothers joy –] must be the sacrifice
To my unhappy beauty?

*Enter Theseus, Hippolyta,* [3] [*Pirithous, and attendants.*]

THESEUS.                    [Bring 'em in
Quickly, by any means; I long to see 'em. –]
Your two contending lovers are returned,
And with them their fair knights; now, my fair sister,
You must love one of them.

EMILIA.                        I had rather both,
So neither for my sake should fall untimely.

THESEUS.
    Who saw 'em?

PIRITHOUS.        I awhile.

[4][GENTLEMAN.]                And I.

*Enter a Messenger.*

THESEUS.
    From whence come you, sir?

MESSENGER.                    From the knights.

THESEUS.                                Pray speak,
    You that have seen them, what they are.

MESSENGER.                            I will, sir,
And truly what I think. Six braver spirits
Than these they have brought – if we judge by the outside –
I never saw, nor read of. He that stands
In the first place with Arcite, by his seeming
Should be a stout man; by his face, a prince.
His very looks so say him; his complexion,
Nearer a brown than black, stern and yet noble,
Which shows him hardy, fearless, proud of dangers;
The circles of his eyes show fire within him,
And as a heated lion, so he looks;
His hair hangs long behind him, black and shining
Like ravens' wings; his shoulders broad and strong,
Armed long and round; and on his thigh a sword
Hung by a curious baldric, when he frowns
To seal his will with – better, o' my conscience,
Was never soldier's friend.

THESEUS.
    Thou hast well described him.

PIRITHOUS.                    Yet a great deal short,
Methinks, of him that's first with Palamon.

THESEUS.
    Pray speak him, friend.

PIRITHOUS.                I guess he is a prince too,
And if it may be, greater; for his show
Has all the ornament of honour in't.
He's somewhat bigger than the knight he spoke of,
But of a face far sweeter; his complexion
Is, as a ripe grape, ruddy; he has felt
Without doubt what he fights for, and so apter
To make this cause his own. In's face appears
All the fair hopes of what he undertakes,
And when he's angry, then a settled valour,
Not tainted with extremes, runs through his body,
And guides his arm to brave things; fear he cannot,
He shows no such soft temper. His head's yellow,
Hard-haired and curled, thick-twined like ivy tods,
Not to undo with thunder; in his face
The livery of the warlike maid appears,

Pure red and white, for yet no beard has blessed him;
[And in his rolling eyes sits victory,
As if she ever meant to court his valour.]
His nose stands high, a character of honour;
His red lips, after fights, are fit for ladies.

EMILIA.
Must these men die too?

PIRITHOUS.                    When he speaks, his tongue
Sounds like a trumpet; all his lineaments
Are as a man would wish 'em, strong and clean;
[He wears a well-steeled axe, the staff of gold;
His age some five-and-twenty.

MESSENGER.                    There's another,
A little man, but of a tough soul, seeming
As great as any; fairer promises
In such a body yet I never looked on.

PIRITHOUS.
O, he that's freckle-faced?

MESSENGER.                    The same, my lord.
Are they not sweet ones?

PIRITHOUS.                    Yes, they are well.

MESSENGER.                    Methinks,
Being so few and well disposed, they show
Great and fine art in Nature. He's white-haired,
Not wanton white, but such a manly colour
Next to an auburn; tough and nimble-set,
Which shows an active soul; his arms are brawny,
Lined with strong sinews; to the shoulder-piece
Gently they swell, like women new-conceived,
Which speaks him prone to labour, never fainting
Under the weight of arms; stout-hearted, still,
But when he stirs, a tiger; he's grey-eyed,
Which yields compassion where he conquers; sharp
To spy advantages, and where he finds 'em,
He's swift to make 'em his; he does no wrongs,
Nor takes none; he's round-faced, and when he smiles
He shows a lover, when he frowns, a soldier;
About his head he wears the winner's oak,
And in it stuck the favour of his lady;
His age some six-and-thirty; in his hand
He bears a charging staff, embossed with silver.]

THESEUS.
Are they all thus?

PIRITHOUS.                    They are all the sons of honour.

THESEUS.
Now, as I have a soul, I long to see 'em!
Lady, you shall see men fight now.

HIPPOLYTA.                    I wish it;
But not the cause, my lord. They would show
Bravely about the titles of two kingdoms;
'Tis pity love should be so tyrannous.
O my soft-hearted sister, what think you?
Weep not till they weep blood, wench; it must be.

THESEUS.
You have steeled 'em with your beauty. – Honoured friend,
To you I give the field; pray order it
Fitting the persons that must use it.

PIRITHOUS.                    Yes, sir.

THESEUS.
Come, I'll go visit 'em; I cannot stay –
Their fame has fired me so – till they appear.
Good friend, be royal.

PIRITHOUS.                    There shall want no bravery.

EMILIA.
Poor wench, go weep, for whosoever wins
Loses a noble cousin for thy sins.

                                        *Exeunt.*

## Scene Three

*Enter Gaoler, Wooer, and Doctor.*

DOCTOR. Her distraction is more at some time of the moon than at
    other some, is it not?

GAOLER. She is continually in a harmless distemper, sleeps little,
    altogether without appetite save often drinking; dreaming of
    another world, and a better; and what broken piece of matter
    soe'er she's about, the name Palamon lards it, that she farces
    every business withal, fits it to every question.

*Enter Gaoler's Daughter.*

Look where she comes; you shall perceive her behaviour.

DAUGHTER. I have forgot it quite; the burden on't was 'down-a,
    down-a', and penned by no worse man than Geraldo, Emilia's
    schoolmaster. He's as fantastical, too, as ever he may go upon's
    legs; for in the next world will Dido see Palamon, and then will
    she be out of love with Aeneas.

[DOCTOR. What stuff's here! Poor soul.

GAOLER. E'en thus all day long.]

DAUGHTER. Now [for this charm that I told you of], you must bring a
piece of silver on the tip of your tongue, or no ferry; then if it be
your chance to come where the blessed spirits are – there's a
sight now! We maids that have our livers perished, cracked to
pieces with love, we shall come there, and do nothing all day
long but pick flowers with Proserpine. Then will I make
Palamon a nosegay; then let him mark me – then –

I

DOCTOR. [How prettily she's amiss!] Note her a little further.

DAUGHTER. [Faith, I'll tell you, sometime we go to barley-break, we
of the blessed.] Alas, 'tis a sore life they have i'th'tother place,
such burning, frying, boiling, hissing, howling, chattering,
cursing – [O, they have shrewd measure; take heed!] If one be
mad, or hang or drown themselves, thither they go [– Jupiter
bless us! –] and there shall we be put in a cauldron of lead and
usurers' grease, amongst a whole million of cutpurses, and
there boil like a gammon of bacon that will never be enough.

DOCTOR. How her brain coins!

DAUGHTER. Lords and courtiers that have got maids with child, they
are in this place; they shall stand in fire up to the navel and in ice
up to th'heart, and there th'offending part burns and the
deceiving part freezes – in troth a very grievous punishment, as
one would think, for such a trifle. Believe me, one would marry
a leprous witch to be rid on't, I'll assure you.

DOCTOR. How she continues this fancy! 'Tis not an engraffed
madness, but a most thick and profound melancholy.

DAUGHTER. To hear there a proud lady and a proud city wife howl
together – I were a beast an I'd call it good sport! One cries 'O,
this smoke!', th'other 'This fire!'; one cries 'O that ever I did it
behind the arras!', and then howls; [th'other curses a suing
fellow and her garden-house.]

*She sings.*

I will be true, my stars, my fate, *etc.*

*Exit.*

GAOLER. What think you of her, sir?

DOCTOR. I think she has a perturbed mind, which I cannot minister
to.

GAOLER. Alas, what then?

DOCTOR. Understand you she ever affected any man ere she beheld
Palamon?

GAOLER. I was once, sir, in great hope she had fixed her liking on this
gentleman my friend.

WOOER. I did think so too, and would account I had a great penn'orth
on't, to give half my state that both she and I at this present
stood unfeignedly on the same terms.

DOCTOR. The intemperate surfeit of her eye hath distempered the
other senses; they may return and settle again [to execute their
preordained faculties,] but they are now in a most extravagant
vagary. This you must do: confine her to a place where the light
may rather seem to steal in than be permitted; take upon you,
young sir her friend, the name of Palamon; say you come to eat
with her and to commune of love. This will catch her attention,
for this her mnd beats upon; other objects that are inserted
'tween her mind and eye become the pranks and friskins of her
madness. Sing to her such green songs of love as she says
Palamon hath sung in prison; come to her stuck in as sweet
flowers as the season is mistress of, [and thereto make an
addition of some other compounded odours, which are grateful
to the sense. All this shall become Palamon, for Palamon can
sing, and Palamon is sweet and every good thing.] Desire to eat
with her, carve her, drink to her, and still among intermingle
your petition of grace and acceptance into her favour. Learn
what maids have been her companions and playferes, and let
them repair to her with Palamon in their mouths, and appear
with tokens, as if they suggested for him. It is a falsehood she is
in, which is with falsehoods to be combated. This may bring
her to eat, to sleep, and reduce what's now out of square in her
into their former law and regiment. I have seen it approved,
how many times I know not, [but to make the number more I
have great hope in this. I will between the passages of this
project come in with my appliance.] Let us put it in excecution,
and hasten the success, which doubt not will bring forth
comfort.

*Exeunt.*

# ACT FIVE

## Scene One

*Flourish. Enter Theseus, Pirithous, Hippolyta, and attendants.*

THESEUS.
    Now let 'em enter, and before the gods
    Tender their holy prayers; let the temples
    Burn bright with sacred fires, and the altars
    In hallowed clouds commend their swelling incense
    To those above us. Let no due be wanting;
    [They have a noble work in hand, will honour
    The very powers that love 'em.]

PIRITHOUS.          Sir, they enter.

*Flourish of cornets. Enter Palamon and Arcite and their knights.*

THESEUS.
    You valiant and strong-hearted enemies,
    You royal german foes, that this day come
    To blow that nearness out that flames between ye,
    Lay by your anger for an hour, and dove-like
    Before the holy altars of your helpers,
    The all-feared gods, bow down your stubborn bodies.
    Your ire is more than mortal; so your help be,
    And as the gods regard ye, fight with justice.
    I'll leave you to your prayers, and betwixt ye
    I part my wishes.

PIRITHOUS.          Honour crown the worthiest!

*Exeunt Theseus, Pirithous, Hippolyta and attendants.*

PALAMON.
    The glass is running now that cannot finish
    Till one of us expire. Think you but thus,
    That were there aught in me which strove to show
    Mine enemy in this business, were't one eye
    Against another, arm oppressed by arm,
    I would destroy th'offender, coz; I would,
    Though parcel of myself. Then from this gather
    How I should tender you.

ARCITE.          I am in labour
    To push your name, your ancient love, our kindred,
    Out of my memory, and i'th'self-same place
    To seat something I would confound. So hoist we
    The sails, that must these vessels port even where
    The heavenly limiter pleases.

PALAMON.          You speak well.
    Before I turn, let me embrace thee, cousin;

*They embrace.*

    This I shall never do again.

ARCITE.          One farewell.

PALAMON.
    Why, let it be so; farewell, coz.

ARCITE.          Farewell, sir.

          *Exeunt Palamon and his knights.*
    Knights, kinsmen, loves – yea, my sacrifices! –
    True worshippers of Mars, [whose spirit in you
    Expels the seeds of fear, and th'apprehension
    Which still is farther off it,] go with me
    Before the god of our profession; there
    Require of him the hearts of lions and
    The breath of tigers, yea, the fierceness too,
    Yea, the speed also – to go on, I mean;
    Else wish we to be snails. You know my prize
    Must be dragged out of blood; force and great feat
    Must put my garland on me, where she sticks,
    The queen of flowers. Our intercession, then,
    Must be to him that makes the camp a cistern
    Brimmed with the blood of men; give me your aid,
    And bend your spirits towards him.

*They prostrate themselves, then kneel before the altar of Mars.*

    Thou mighty one, [that with thy power hast turned
    Green Neptune into purple, whose approach
    Comets prewarn,] whose havoc in vast field
    Unearthèd skulls proclaim, whose breath blows down
    The teeming Ceres' foison, who dost pluck
    With hand armipotent from forth blue clouds
    The masoned turrets, that both makest and breakest
    The stony girths of cities; me thy pupil,
    Youngest follower of thy drum, instruct this day
    With military skill, that to thy laud
    I may advance my streamer, and by thee
    Be styled the lord o'th'day; give me, great Mars,
    Some token of thy pleasure.

*Here they fall on their faces as formerly, and there is heard clanging of armour, with a short thunder as the burst of a battle, whereupon they all rise and bow to the altar.*

    O great corrector of enormous times,
    Shaker of o'er-rank states, [thou grand decider
    Of dusty and old titles,] that healest with blood

The earth when it is sick, and curest the world
O'th'plurisy of people; I do take
Thy signs auspiciously, and in thy name
To my design march boldy. Let us go.

*Exeunt Arcite and his knights.*
*Enter Palamon and his knights, with the former observance.*

PALAMON.

Our stars must glister with new fire, or be
Today extinct; our argument is love,
Which if the goddess of it grant, she gives
Victory too. [1][Then blend your spirits with mine,
You whose free nobleness do make my cause
Your personal hazard;] to the goddess Venus
Commend we our proceeding, and implore
Her power unto our party.

*Here they prostrate themselves, then kneel as formerly to the altar of Venus.*

Hail, sovereign queen of secrets, who hast power
To call the fiercest tyrant from his rage
And weep unto a girl; that hast the might
Even with an eye-glance to choke Mars's drum
And turn th'alarm to whispers; that canst make
A cripple flourish with his crutch, and cure him
Before Apollo; that mayst force the king
To be his subject's vassal, and induce
Stale gravity to dance; [the polled bachelor,
Whose youth, like wanton boys through bonfires,
Have skipped thy flame, at seventy thou canst catch,
And make him, to the scorn of his hoarse throat,
Abuse young lays of love.] What godlike power
Hast thou not power upon? [To Phoebus thou
Addest flames hotter than his; the heavenly fires
Did scorch his mortal son, thine him; the huntress
All moist and cold, some say began to throw
Her bow away and sigh.] Take to thy grace
Me thy vowed soldier, who do bear thy yoke
As 'twere a wreath of roses, yet is heavier
Than lead itself, stings more than nettles.
I have never been foul-mouthed against thy law;
Ne'er revealed secret, [for I knew none; would not,
Had I kenned all that were;] I never practised
Upon man's wife, nor would the libels read
Of liberal wits; I never at great feasts
Sought to betray a beauty, but have blushed
At simpering sirs that did; I have been harsh
To large confessors, and have hotly asked them
If they had mothers – I had one, a woman,
And women 'twere they wronged. I knew a man
Of eighty winters – this I told them – who
A lass of fourteen brided. 'Twas thy power
To put life into dust; the agèd cramp
Had screwed his square foot round,
The gout had knit his fingers into knots,
Torturing convulsions from his globy eyes
Had almost drawn their spheres, that what was life
In him seemed torture. This anatomy
Had by his young fair fere a boy, and I
Believed it was his, for she swore it was,
And who would not believe her? [Brief, I am
To those that prate and have done, no companion;
To those that boast and have not, a defier;
To those that would and cannot, a rejoicer.
Yea, him I do not love that tells close offices
The foulest way, nor names concealments in
The boldest language; such a one I am,
And][2] vow that lover never yet made sigh
Truer than I. O then, most soft sweet goddess,
Give me the victory of this question, which
Is true love's merit, and bless me with a sign
Of thy great pleasure.

*Here music is heard and doves are seen to flutter. They fall again*
*upon their faces, then on their knees.*

O thou that from eleven to ninety reignest
In mortal bosoms, whose chase is this world
And we in herds thy game, I give thee thanks
For this fair token, which, being laid unto
Mine innocent true heart, arms in assurance
My body to this business. Let us rise
And bow before the goddess.

*They bow.*

Time comes on.

*Exeunt Palamon and his knights.*

*Still music of records. Enter Emilia in white, her hair about her*
*shoulders, with a wheaten wreath; one in white holding up her train,*
*her hair stuck with flowers; one before her carrying a silver hind, in*
*which is conveyed incense and sweet odours; which being set upon*
*the altar of Diana, her maids standing aloof, she sets fire to it. Then*
*they curtsy and kneel.*

EMILIA.

O sacred, shadowy, cold, and constant queen,
Abandoner of revels, mute contemplative,
Sweet, solitary, white as chaste, and pure

As wind-fanned snow, [3][who to thy female knights
Allowest no more blood than will make a blush,
Which is their order's robe; I here, thy priest,
Am humbled 'fore thine altar. O, vouchsafe
With that thy rare green eye, which never yet
Beheld thing maculate, look on thy virgin;
And, sacred silver mistress, lend thine ear –
Which ne'er heard scurril term, into whose port
Ne'er entered wanton sound – to my petition]
Seasoned with holy fear. This is my last
Of vestal office; I am bride-habited,
But maiden-hearted; a husband I have 'pointed,
But do not know him. Out of two I should
Choose one, and pray for his success, but I
Am guiltless of election. Of mine eyes
Were I to lose one, they are equal precious,
I could doom neither; [that which perished should
Go to't unsentenced. Therefore,][4] most modest queen,
He of the two pretenders that best loves me
And has the truest title in't, let him
Take off my wheaten garland, or else grant
The file and quality I hold I may
Continue in thy band.

*Here the hind vanishes under the altar, and in the place ascends a rose tree, having one rose upon it.*

See what our general of ebbs and flows
Out from the bowels of her holy altar
With sacred act advances: but one rose!
If well inspired, this battle shall confound
Both these brave knights, and I a virgin flower
Must grow alone, unplucked.

*Here is heard a sudden twang of instruments, and the rose falls from the tree.*

The flower is fallen, the tree descends! O mistress,
Thou here dischargest me; I shall be gathered;
I think so, but I know not thine own will;
Unclasp thy mystery. – I hope she's pleased;
Her signs were gracious.

*They curtsy and exeunt.*

## Scene Two

*Enter Doctor, Gaoler, and Wooer in habit of Palamon.*

DOCTOR.
Has this advice I told you done any good upon her?

WOOER.
O, very much. The maids that kept her company
Have half persuaded her that I am Palamon;
Within this half hour she came smiling to me,
And asked me what I would eat, and when I would kiss her.
I told her, presently, and kissed her twice.

DOCTOR.
'Twas well done; twenty times had been far better,
For there the cure lies mainly.

WOOER.                              Then she told me
She would watch with me tonight, for well she knew
What hour my fit would take me.

DOCTOR.                              Let her do so,
And when your fit comes, fit her home, and presently.

WOOER.
She would have me sing.

DOCTOR.                    You did so?

WOOER.                                   No.

DOCTOR.                                         'Twas very ill done, then;
You should observe her every way.

WOOER.                                 Alas,
I have no voice, sir, to confirm her that way.

DOCTOR.
That's all one, if ye make a noise.
If she entreat again, do anything;
Lie with her if she ask you.

GAOLER.                        Ho there, doctor!

DOCTOR.
Yes, in the way of cure.

GAOLER.                     But first, by your leave,
I'th'way of honesty.

DOCTOR.              That's but a niceness.
Ne'er cast your child away for honesty;
Cure her first this way, then if she will be honest,
She has the path before her.

GAOLER.                        Thank ye, doctor.

DOCTOR.
Pray bring her in and let's see how she is.

GAOLER.
I will, and tell her her Palamon stays for her.
But, doctor, methinks you are i'th'wrong still.

*Exit.*

DOCTOR.                                        Go, go.
You fathers are fine fools! Her honesty?
An we should give her physic till we find that –

WOOER.
Why, do you think she is not honest, sir?

DOCTOR.
How old is she?

WOOER.                    She's eighteen.

DOCTOR.                                        She may be –
But that's all one, 'tis nothing to our purpose.
Whate'er her father says, if you perceive
Her mood inclining that way that I spoke of,
*Videlicet,* the way of flesh – you have me?

WOOER.
Yet very well, sir.

DOCTOR.                    Please her appetite,
And do it home; it cures her *ipso facto*
The melancholy humour that infects her.

WOOER.
I am of your mind, doctor.

*Enter Gaoler, Gaoler's Daughter, and her maid.*

DOCTOR.
You'll find it so. She comes; pray humour her.

GAOLER.
Come, your love Palamon stays for you, child,
And has done this long hour, to visit you.

DAUGHTER.
I thank him for his gentle patience;
He's a kind gentleman, and I am much bound to him.
Did you ne'er see the horse he gave me?

GAOLER.                                        Yes.

DAUGHTER.
How do you like him?

GAOLER.                    He's a very fair one.

DAUGHTER.
You never saw him dance?

GAOLER.                                        No.

DAUGHTER.                    I have often.
He dances very finely, very comely,
And for a jig, come cut and long tail to him,
He turns ye like a top.

GAOLER.                    That's fine indeed.

DAUGHTER.
He'll dance the morris twenty mile an hour,
And that will founder the best hobby-horse,
If I have any skill, in all the parish;
And gallops to the tune of 'Light o'Love'.
What think you of this horse?

GAOLER.                                        Having these virtues,
I think he might be brought to play at tennis.

DAUGHTER.
Alas, that's nothing.

GAOLER.                    Can he write and read too?

DAUGHTER.
A very fair hand, and casts himself th'accounts
Of all his hay and provender; that ostler
Must rise betime that cozens him. You know
The chestnut mare the Duke has?

GAOLER.                                        Very well.

DAUGHTER.
She is horribly in love with him, poor beast,
But he is like his master, coy and scornful.

GAOLER.
What dowry has she?

DAUGHTER.                    Some two hundred bottles,
And twenty strike of oats; but he'll ne'er have her.
He lisps in's neighing able to entice
A miller's mare. He'll be the death of her.

DOCTOR.
What stuff she utters!

GAOLER.
Make curtsy, here your love comes.

WOOER (*comes forward*).                    Pretty soul,
How do ye? That's a fine maid; there's a curtsy!

DAUGHTER.
Yours to command i'th'way of honesty.
How far is't now to th'end o'th'world, my masters?

DOCTOR.
Why, a day's journey, wench.

DAUGHTER (*to Wooer*).                Will you go there with me?

WOOER.
What shall we do there, wench?

DAUGHTER.                     Why, play at stool-ball.
What is there else to do?

WOOER.                 I am content,
If we shall keep our wedding there.

DAUGHTER.                     'Tis true;
For there, I will assure you, we shall find
Some blind priest for the purpose, that will venture
To marry us, for here they are nice and foolish.
Besides, my father must be hanged tomorrow,
And that would be a blot i'th'business.
Are you not Palamon?

WOOER.            Do not you know me?

DAUGHTER.
Yes, but you care not for me; I have nothing
But this poor petticoat and two coarse smocks.

WOOER.
That's all one; I will have you.

DAUGHTER.            Will you surely?

WOOER.
Yes, by this fair hand will I.

DAUGHTER.            We'll to bed then.

WOOER.
E'en when you will.

*He kisses her.*

DAUGHTER.            O sir, you would fain be nibbling.

WOOER.
Why do you rub my kiss off?

DAUGHTER.               'Tis a sweet one,
And will perfume me finely against the wedding.
Is not this your cousin Arcite?

DOCTOR.            Yes, sweetheart,
And I am glad my cousin Palamon
Has made so fair a choice.

DAUGHTER.            Do you think he'll have me?

DOCTOR.
Yes, without doubt.

DAUGHTER.            Do you think so too?

GAOLER.                     Yes.

DAUGHTER.
We shall have many children. – Lord, how you're grown!
My Palamon I hope will grow too, finely,
Now he's at liberty. Alas, poor chicken,
He was kept down with hard meat and ill lodging;
But I'll kiss him up again.

*Enter a Messenger.*

MESSENGER.
What do you do here? You'll lose the noblest sight
That e'er was seen.

GAOLER.            Are they i'th'field?

MESSENGER.                     They are.
You bear a charge there too.

GAOLER.               I'll away straight.
I must e'en leave you here.

DOCTOR.            Nay, we'll go with you.
I will not lose the fight.

GAOLER.            How did you like her?

DOCTOR.
I'll warrant you, within these three or four days
I'll make her right again. (*To Wooer:*) You must not from her,
But still preserve her in this way.

WOOER.                     I will.

DOCTOR.
Let's get her in.

WOOER.         Come, sweet, we'll go to dinner,
And then we'll play at cards.

DAUGHTER.            And shall we kiss too?

WOOER.
A hundred times.

DAUGHTER.         – And twenty.

WOOER.                     Ay, and twenty.

DAUGHTER.
And then we'll sleep together.

DOCTOR.            Take her offer.

WOOER.
  Yes, marry, will we.

DAUGHTER.          But you shall not hurt me.

WOOER.
  I will not, sweet.

DAUGHTER.          If you do, love, I'll cry.

                                        *Exeunt.*


## Scene Three

*Flourish. Enter Theseus, Hippolyta, Emilia, Pirithous, and some attendants.*

EMILIA.
  I'll no step further.

PIRITHOUS.          Will you lose this sight?

EMILIA.
  I had rather see a wren hawk at a fly
  Than this decision. Every blow that falls
  Threats a brave life; each stroke laments
  The place whereon it falls, and sounds more like
  A bell than blade. I will stay here.
  It is enough my hearing shall be punished
  With what shall happen, ['gainst the which there is
  No deafing, but to hear; not taint mine eye
  With dread sights it may shun.]

PIRITHOUS.                Sir, my good lord,
  Your sister will no further.

THESEUS.            [O, she must;
  She shall see deeds of honour in their kind
  Which sometime show well pencilled. Nature now
  Shall make and act the story, the belief
  Both sealed with eye and ear.] (*To Emilia:*) You must be present;
  You are the victor's meed, the prize and garland
  To crown the question's title.

EMILIA.          Pardon me;
  If I were there, I'd wink.

THESEUS.          You must be there;
  This trial is as 'twere i'th'night, and you
  The only star to shine.

EMILIA.          I am extinct.

There is but envy in that light which shows
The one the other; darkness, which ever was
The dam of horror, who does stand accursed
Of many mortal millions, may even now,
By casting her black mantle over both,
That neither could find other, get herself
Some part of a good name, and many a murder
Set off whereto she's guilty.

HIPPOLYTA.          You must go.

EMILIA.
  In faith, I will not.

THESEUS.          Why, the knights must kindle
  Their valour at your eye; know of this war
  You are the treasure, and must needs be by
  To give the service pay.

EMILIA.          Sir, pardon me;
  The title of a kingdom may be tried
  Out of itself.

THESEUS.          Well, well, then, at your pleasure.
  Those that remain with you could wish their office
  To any of their enemies.

HIPPOLYTA.          Farewell, sister;
  I am like to know your husband 'fore yourself
  By some small start of time. He whom the gods
  Do of the two know best, I pray them he
  Be made your lot.

              *All go out except Emilia and her attendants.*

EMILIA.
  Arcite is gently visaged, yet his eye
  Is like an engine bent or a sharp weapon
  In a soft sheath; mercy and manly courage
  Are bedfellows in his visage. Palamon
  Has a most menacing aspect; his brow
  Is graved, and seems to bury what it frowns on.
  Yet sometime 'tis not so, but alters to
  The quality of his thoughts; long time his eye
  Will dwell upon his object. Melancholy
  Becomes him nobly; so does Arcite's mirth,
  [But Palamon's sadness is a kind of mirth,
  So mingled as if mirth did make him sad,
  And sadness merry. Those darker humours that
  Stick misbecomingly on others, on him
  Live in fair dwelling.]

*Cornets. Trumpets sound as to a charge.*

Hark how yon spurs to spirit do incite
The princes to their proof! Arcite may win me,
And yet may Palamon wound Arcite to
The spoiling of his figure. O, what pity
Enough for such a chance? If I were by,
I might do hurt, for they would glance their eyes
Toward my seat, and in that motion might
Omit a ward or forfeit an offence
Which craved that very time. It is much better
I am not there – O, better never born,
Than minister to such harm!

*Cornets. A great cry and noise within, crying* 'A Palamon!' *Enter a Servant.*

                        What is the chance?

SERVANT.
The cry's 'A Palamon!'

EMILIA.
Then he has won. 'Twas ever likely;
He looked all grace and success, and he is
Doubtless the primest of men. I prithee run
And tell me how it goes.

*Shouts and cornets, crying* 'A Palamon!'

SERVANT.                 Still Palamon.

EMILIA.
Run and inquire.

                                    *Exit Servant.*

                    Poor servant, thou hast lost!
Upon my right side still I wore thy picture,
Palamon's on the left – why so, I know not,
I had no end in't; else chance would have it so.
On the sinister side the heart lies; Palamon
Had the best-boding chance.

*Another cry, and shout within, and cornets.*

                    This burst of clamour
Is sure th'end o'th'combat.

*Enter Servant.*

SERVANT.
They said that Palamon had Arcite's body
Within an inch o'th'pyramid, that the cry
Was general 'A Palamon!' But anon
Th'assistants made a brave redemption, and
The two bold titlers at this instant are

Hand to hand at it.

EMILIA.                    Were they metamorphosed
Both into one! O, why, there were no woman
Worth so composed a man; [their single share,
Their nobleness peculiar to them, gives
The prejudice of disparity, value's shortness,
To any lady breathing –]

*Cornets. Cry within* 'Arcite, Arcite!'

                        More exulting?
'Palamon' still?

SERVANT.                 Nay, now the sound is 'Arcite'.

EMILIA.
I prithee lay attention to the cry;
Set both thine ears to th'business.

*Cornets. A great shout and cry* 'Arcite, victory!'

SERVANT.                            The cry is
'Arcite' and 'Victory!' Hark, 'Arcite, victory!'
[The combat's consummation is proclaimed
By the wind instruments.]

EMILIA.                    Half-sights saw
That Arcite was no babe – God's lid, his richness
And costliness of spirit looked through him; it could
No more be hid in him than fire in flax,
[Than humble banks can go to law with waters
That drift winds force to raging. I did think
Good Palamon would miscarry, yet I knew not
Why I did think so; our reasons are not prophets
When oft our fancies are.]

*Cornets.*

                        They are coming off.
Alas, poor Palamon!

*Enter Theseus, Hippolyta, Pirithous, Arcite as victor, and attendants.*

THESEUS.
Lo, where our sister is in expectation,
Yet quaking and unsettled! – Fairest Emily,
The gods by their divine arbitrament
Have given you this knight; he is a good one
As ever struck at head. Give me your hands.
Receive you her, you him; be plighted with
A love that grows as you decay.

ARCITE.                                    Emilia,
  To buy you I have lost what's dearest to me
  Save what is bought, and yet I purchase cheaply,
  As I do rate your value.

THESEUS.                              O loved sister,
  He speaks now of as brave a knight as e'er
  Did spur a noble steed; surely the gods
  Would have him die a bachelor, lest his race
  [1][Should show i'th'world too godlike! His behaviour
  So charmed me that methought Alcides was
  To him a sow of lead.] If I could praise
  Each part of him to th'all I have spoke, your Arcite
  Did not lose by't; for he that was thus good
  Encountered yet his better. I have heard
  Two emulous Philomels beat the ear o'th'night
  With their contentious throats, now one the higher,
  Anon the other, then again the first,
  And by and by outbreasted, that the sense
  Could not be judge between 'em; so it fared
  Good space between these kinsmen, till heavens did
  Make hardly one the winner. – Wear the garland
  With joy that you have won. – For the subdued,
  Give them our present justice, since I know
  Their lives but [2][pinch] 'em; let it here be done.
  The scene's not for our seeing; go we hence,
  Right joyful, with some sorrow. (*To Arcite*:) Arm your prize;
  I know you will not lose her.

*Arcite takes Emilia's arm in his. Flourish.*

                       Hippolyta,
  I see one eye of yours conceives a tear,
  The which it will deliver.

EMILIA.                              Is this winning?
  O all you heavenly powers, where is your mercy?
  But that your wills have said it must be so,
  And charge me live to comfort this unfriended,
  This miserable prince, that cuts away
  A life more worthy from him than all women,
  I should, and would, die too.

HIPPOLYTA.                          Infinite pity
  That four such eyes should be so fixed on one
  That two must needs be blind for't.

THESEUS.                              So it is.

                               *Exeunt.*

## Scene Four

*Enter Palamon and his knights pinioned, with Gaoler, executioner, and a guard of soldiers.*

PALAMON.
  There's many a man alive that hath outlived
  The love o'th'people; yea, [i'th'selfsame state
  Stands many a father with his child;] some comfort
  We have by so considering. [We expire,
  And not without men's pity; to live still,
  Have their good wishes.] We prevent
  That loathsome misery of age, beguile
  The gout and rheum, [that in lag hours attend
  For grey approachers;] we come towards the gods
  Young and unwappered, not halting under crimes
  Many and stale; that sure shall please the gods
  Sooner than such, to give us nectar with 'em,
  For we are more clear spirits. My dear kinsmen,
  Whose lives for this poor comfort are laid down,
  You have sold 'em too too cheap.

FIRST KNIGHT.                    What ending could be
  Of more content? O'er us the victors have
  Fortune, whose title is as momentary
  As to us death is certain; [a grain of honour
  They not o'erweigh us.]

SECOND KNIGHT.                  Let us bid farewell,
  And with our patience anger tottering fortune,
  Who at her certain'st reels.

THIRD KNIGHT.                    Come, who begins?

PALAMON.
  E'en he that led you to this banquet shall
  Taste to you all. (*To Gaoler*:) Aha, my friend, my friend,
  Your gentle daughter gave me freedom once;
  You'll see't done now for ever. Pray, how does she?
  I heard she was not well; her kind of ill
  Gave me some sorrow.

GAOLER.                          Sir, she's well restored,
  And to be married shortly.

PALAMON.                        By my short life,
  I am most glad on't; 'tis the latest thing
  I shall be glad of. Prithee tell her so;
  Commend me to her, and to piece her portion
  Tender her this.

*He gives Gaoler his purse.*

FIRST KNIGHT.        Nay, let's be offerers all.

SECOND KNIGHT.
    Is it a maid?

PALAMON.        Verily I think so;
    A right good creature, more to me deserving
    Than I can quite or speak of.

ALL THREE KNIGHTS.        Commend us to her.

    *They give their purses.*

GAOLER.
    The gods requite you all, and make her thankful.

PALAMON.
    Adieu; and let my life be now as short
    As my leave-taking.

FIRST KNIGHT.        Lead, courageous cousin.

SECOND KNIGHT.
    We'll follow cheerfully.

    *Palamon lies on the block. A great noise within, crying* 'Run! Save!
    Hold!' *Enter in haste a Messenger.*

[1][MESSENGER.]
    Hold, hold, [O hold, hold, hold!]

    *Enter Pirithous in haste.*

PIRITHOUS.
    Hold, ho! It is a cursèd haste you made
    If you have done so quickly. Noble Palamon,
    The gods will show their glory in a life
    That thou art yet to lead.

PALAMON.        Can that be, when
    Venus I have said is false? How do things fare?

PIRITHOUS.
    Arise, great sir, and give the tidings ear
    That are most early sweet and bitter.

PALAMON.        What
    Hath waked us from our dream?

PIRITHOUS.        List then. Your cousin,
    Mounted upon a steed that Emily
    Did first bestow on him, a black one, owing
    Not a hair-worth of white, which some will say
    Weakens his price, and many will not buy
    His goodness with this note – which superstition
    Here finds allowance – on this horse is Arcite
    Trotting the stones of Athens, which the calkins
    Did rather tell than trample, for the horse

    Would make his length a mile, if't pleased his rider
    To put pride in him. As he thus went counting
    The flinty pavement, dancing as 'twere to th'music
    His own hooves made – for, as they say, from iron
    Came music's origin – what envious flint,
    Cold as old Saturn and like him possessed
    With fire malevolent, darted a spark,
    Or what fierce sulphur else, to this end made,
    I comment not; the hot horse, hot as fire,
    Took toy at this, and fell to what disorder
    His power could give his will – bounds, comes on end,
    Forgets school-doing, [being therein trained
    And of kind manage;] pig-like he whines
    At the sharp rowel, [which he frets at rather
    Than any jot obeys;] seeks all foul means
    Of boisterous and rough jadery to disseat
    His lord, that kept it bravely. When naught served,
    When neither curb would crack, girth break, nor differing
        plunges
    Disroot his rider whence he grew, but that
    He kept him 'tween his legs, on his hind hooves
    On end he stands,
    That Arcite's legs, being higher than his head,
    Seemed with strange art to hang; his victor's wreath
    Even then fell off his head; and presently
    Backward the jade comes o'er, and his full poise
    Becomes the rider's load. Yet is he living;
    But such a vessel 'tis that floats but for
    The surge that next approaches. He much desires
    To have some speech with you. Lo, he appears.

    *Enter Theseus, Hippolyta, Emilia, and Arcite carried in a chair.*

PALAMON.
    O miserable end of our alliance!
    The gods are mighty. Arcite, if thy heart,
    Thy worthy, manly heart, be yet unbroken,
    Give me thy last words. I am Palamon,
    One that yet loves thee dying.

ARCITE.        Take Emilia,
    And with her all the world's joy; reach thy hand.
    Farewell; I have told my last hour. I was false,
    Yet never treacherous; forgive me, cousin.
    One kiss from fair Emilia –

    *She kisses him.*

        'Tis done.
    Take her; I die.

        *He dies.*

PALAMON.                    Thy brave soul seek Elysium!

EMILIA.
    I'll close thine eyes, prince; blessèd souls be with thee!
    Thou art a right good man, and while I live
    This day I give to tears.

PALAMON.                          And I to honour.

THESEUS.
    In this place first you fought; e'en very here
    I sundered you. Acknowledge to the gods
    Your thanks that you are living.
    His part is played, and though it were too short
    He did it well; your day is lengthened, and
    The blissful dew of heaven does arrouse you.
    The powerful Venus well hath graced her altar,
    And given you your love; our master Mars
    Hath vouched his oracle, and to Arcite gave
    The grace of the contention; so the deities
    Have showed due justice. Bear this hence.

PALAMON.                            O cousin,
    That we should things desire which do cost us
    The loss of our desire! That naught could buy
    Dear love but loss of dear love!

THESEUS.                          Never fortune
    Did play a subtler game: the conquered triumphs,
    The victor has the loss; yet in the passage
    The gods have been most equal. Palamon,
    Your kinsman hath confessed the right o'th'lady
    Did lie in you, for you first saw her, and
    Even then proclaimed your fancy; he restored her
    As your stolen jewel, and desired your spirit
    To send him hence forgiven. The gods my justice
    Take from my hand, and they themselves become
    The executioners. Lead your lady off;
    And call your lovers from the stage of death,
    Whom I adopt my friends. A day or two
    Let us look sadly, and give grace unto
    The funeral of Arcite, in whose end
    The visages of bridegrooms we'll put on
    And smile with Palamon; for whom an hour,
    But one hour since, I was as dearly sorry
    As glad of Arcite, and am now as glad
    As for him sorry. O you heavenly charmers,
    What things you make of us! For what we lack
    We laugh; for what we have are sorry; still
    Are children in some kind. Let us be thankful
    For that which is, and with you leave dispute
    That are above our question. Let's go off,
    And bear us like the time.

                                *Flourish. Exeunt.*

## EPILOGUE

    I would now ask ye how ye like the play,
    But, as it is with schoolboys, cannot say;
    I am cruel fearful. Pray yet stay awhile,
    And let me look upon ye. No man smile?
    Then it goes hard, I see. He that has
    Loved a young handsome wench, then, show his face –
    'Tis strange if none be here – and if he will
    Against his conscience, let him hiss, and kill
    Our market. 'Tis in vain, I see, to stay ye.
    Have at the worst can come, then! Now, what say ye?
    And yet mistake me not. I am not bold;
    We have no such cause. If the tale we have told –
    For 'tis no other – any way content ye,
    For to that honest purpose it was meant ye,
    We have our end; and ye shall have ere long
    I dare say many a better, to prolong
    Your old loves to us. We, and all our might,
    Rest at your service. Gentlemen, good night.

                                *Flourish. Exit.*

# Endnotes

**ACT ONE**
**Scene One**
1 Show pity, to us!
2 Then
3 *Insert:* glass of ladies
4 Lord,
5 Come
**Scene Two**
1 Make
2 others'
3 men's
4 and
5 any
6 and such a case is ours
7 Since
**Scene Three**
1 say our hearts
2           Have you observed him much
Since our great lord departed? How his longing
Follows his friend! Since that depart, his sports,
Though craving seriousness and skill, passed slightly
With careless execution.
HIPPOLYTA.
      And I do love him for't. They two have cabined
      In many a corner as dangerous as poor,
      Peril and want contending; they have skiffed
      Torrents whose tyranny and power do dread
      And fought together where death's self was lodged;
      Yet fate hath brought them off. Their knot of love,
      Tied, weaved, entangled, is so true, so long;
      It cannot be outworn, never undone.
3 *Insert:* of years
4 story
**Scene Four**
1 *Insert: Pirithous*
2 May
3 aPIRITHOUS.
      Men of great quality.
HERALD.           Wi'leave, they're called
      Arcite and Palamon
4 By th'helm of Mars, I saw them in the war,
Like a pair of lions, smeared with prey,
Make lanes in troops aghast. I fixed my note
Constantly on them, for they were a mark
Worth a god's view.
5 with speed

## ACT TWO
**Scene One**
1 Is there
**Scene Two**
1 he'll
2 THIRD COUNTRYMAN. Do we hold against the maying?
3 sempster's
**Scene Five**
1 well

## ACT THREE
**Scene One**
1 that has
**Scene Five**
1 THIRD.
2 women?
3 FOURTH COUNTRYMAN.
    Here's
4 SECOND.
5 FIRST COUNTRYMAN.
    We may go whistle.
FOURTH COUNTRYMAN.
              All the fat's i'th'fire.
6 FIRST.
7 SECOND.
8 FOURTH.
**Scene Six**
1 the blood that
2 *Insert:* So
3 If unto neither thou do show thy mercy.

## ACT FOUR
**Scene One**
1 WOOER.
**Scene Two**
1 Palamon is but his foil; a mere shadow.
2 PIRITHOUS.
3 *and Artesius.*
4 ARTESIUS.
**Scene Three**
1 *Insert:* DOCTOR. What stuff's here! Poor soul.
    GAOLER. E'en thus all day long.

## ACT FIVE
**Scene One**
1 Thus

2 I
3     O look upon thy virgin;
    And, lend thine ear – to her petition
4 Thus
**Scene Three**
1 show th'world too godlike!
2 pain
**Scene Four**
GAOLER.